Creating Speeches:
A Decision-Making Approach

Third Edition

Nancy Goulden
William Schenck-Hamlin

HAYDEN
HM
McNEIL

Printed in the United States of America

10 9 8 7 6 5 4 3 2 1

ISBN 978-0-7380-3616-8

Hayden-McNeil Publishing
14903 Pilot Drive
Plymouth, MI 48170
www.hmpublishing.com

Brazeal 3616-8 F09

TABLE OF CONTENTS

Introduction

The educated individual not only possesses knowledge, but is also able to communicate that knowledge effectively to others. Education is not complete until a person can speak clearly and convincingly in public situations, listen critically, and respond intelligently to the messages of others. Acknowledging the importance of these skills to a liberal education, the Association for American Colleges includes speaking and listening in its inventory of basic literacy skills along with reading and writing.

Surveys of American business and industry have repeatedly demonstrated the importance high-level executives attach to communication skills. A recent study published in *Job Outlook '96* reported that responding employers ranked oral communication number one above such skills as "leadership skills" and even "proficiency in field of study." According to *Engineering Education*, speaking and writing skills are listed as "very important" by professional engineers more often than any other job-related competency. Numerous surveys have linked improved communication skills to increased job efficiency and productivity. In addition, many careers such as teaching, the ministry, sales, law, and consulting are fundamentally communication-oriented. Indeed, research indicates that the frequency with which all of us are required to make formal presentations increases with our education level.

Off the job, speaking and listening skills enhance one's ability to take an active part in social and community affairs. Participation in civic and religious organizations, political activities, public hearings, charity fundraisers, etc., is the birthright and responsibility of every citizen in a democratic society. The acquisition of speechmaking skills will help an individual to participate more intelligently in the public arena.

The ability to present one's ideas effectively and to respond intelligently to the ideas of others, whether on or off the job, is clearly desirable to the educated person. This course proceeds from the well-established premise that such ability can be acquired through training, practice, and hard work. Effective public communicators are not an especially "gifted" class of people, but they are people who have consciously mastered the skills necessary to be comfortable and proficient in this sphere of human activity. Public Speaking is designed to help students develop and refine these important skills.

Public Speaking and Decision Making

CHAPTER **1**
Studying Public Speaking

Chapter Objectives
After reading the chapter you should be able to:
• Recognize that you have knowledge and understanding of Public Speaking.
• Have a general understanding of the process of speech building and how that process will be taught in the course.
• Identify the relationships of speechmaking decisions and factors that influence those decisions.

Starting with What You Know about Public Speaking

As you begin this course on Public Speaking, you already have had a great deal of experience listening to speeches, such as class lectures, sermons, guest lectures, banquet speeches, and job training lectures. No doubt you also have some insight into what makes a "good" speech and what makes a "weak" speech. The following statements and questions will allow you to recall and analyze elements of public speaking that have significant impact on the quality of speeches.

ACTIVITY **1.1**
Thinking about Public Speeches

1. List three prepared live speeches you have heard in the last two months. The types of speeches listed on the previous page (class lectures, sermons, guest lectures) are appropriate examples of public speeches.

2. Think about the content of each of the speeches. Can you write a brief outline of the content of any of the speeches?

3. Concentrate now on specific details (stories, examples, statistics, comparisons, descriptions, facts) you can remember from one of the speeches. Jot down specific information from the speech.

4. What visual images created by the speaker's words do you remember from any of the speeches?

5. Write one new thing you learned from any one of the speeches.

6. List three characteristics of the "good" or "better" speeches.

7. What would have improved any of the speeches for you?

8. List three areas of speechmaking you would like to improve this semester.

Plan of Course

There are many different ways that a course in public speaking can be developed. We believe the most useful approach for college students is to focus on **how to prepare a speech**. Concentrating on the preparation of the speech is beneficial in a first public speaking course, because students learn a general process of speech building that they can use for creating speeches outside of the classroom based on different requirements and different situations. By understanding speech building and the skills that are necessary for preparing effective speeches, students will also be able to apply what they have learned about managing information for speeches to other communication contexts such as writing papers, working on group projects and reports, and even responding orally in class discussions.

The **process of speech preparation** has much in common with other processes. We are going to compare the process of building a house to the process of constructing a speech as a way to explain the topics that will be studied in this course and the order that we plan to cover those topics.

No decisions about building a house can be made until the builder has investigated certain factors that may limit what can be done. The builder must inventory such things as financial resources, local building and zoning codes, the topography, and boundaries of the land. In speech building also, the builder begins by surveying what is possible and what will limit the speaker's range of choices. Students in this course begin studying public speaking by looking at the specific speaking situation and how certain aspects, which we label as **Decision Factors**, shape the speakers' decisions.

After the builder has reviewed important factors that will affect choices, the next step in planning the house is to make the major decisions about the house:

Where on the property will the house be located?

What type of structure will it be—stone? wood? log?

How big will the house be?

In speechmaking, there are also significant decisions that determine the overall shape and texture of the speech, such as: topic selection, goal of speech, and organization of the material. In this course, the major speech construction decisions are given the title of **Global Decisions**.

For example, once the builder has decided that the new house will have three rooms and a bathroom, will be made of wood, and will be an A-frame, the builder is then ready to make more specific decisions that apply to only one part of the house, such as a stone fireplace in the living room, putting a shower in the bathroom, and placing the kitchen sink under a window. Speechmakers also have decisions to make that affect only part of the speech:

How to word the first sentence of the introduction?

What statistics to include?

Where to stand when presenting the speech?

These are **Local Decisions.**

In this course, you will study first about Decision Factors that influence and limit speechmaking decisions; next you will learn about Global Decisions that guide the creation and development of the entire speech; then you will be introduced to the Local Decisions that are specific to only one part of the speech. After a student has studied these three major topics, it might appear that the student has learned all there is to learn about speech building and would then work independently to create speeches.

The experience of being introduced to Decision Factors, Global Decisions, and Local Decisions does give students a good general understanding of how to go about constructing a speech, but we have discovered that students need more instruction and practice with the type of Local Decisions known as **Support Materials** before they can successfully create a major researched speech. Just as someone building a house might be able to make the Global and Local Decisions without further instruction, they probably would not be able to build the house unless they spent some time learning and practicing specific skills such as plumbing, electrical installation, stone masonry, and woodworking. You will find that much of the course focuses on learning and practicing the skills of speech construction by working with a series of support materials that are the analogies of the house-building skills.

The Support Materials covered in the course are (a) Narration, (b) Definition, (c) Description, (d) Comparison, (e) Memorization, (f) Evidence, and (g) Argument. Support Materials can be used any place in a speech from introduction to conclusion and within the body of the speech. The final portion of the course is based on speaking assignments that require the speaker to integrate what has been learned about *Decision Factors, Global Decisions, Local Decisions*, and *Support Materials* in order to construct major speeches.

You may have noticed that we have not included the skills of delivering or presenting a speech as part of the process. Delivery certainly contributes to the impact of the speech; however, the success of any speech depends first and foremost on the planning and content of the speech itself, just as a strong, pleasing house depends on the materials and design of the building itself. A house can be enhanced by interior and exterior decorating and landscaping, just as a speech can be improved by enthusiastic delivery free from distracting behaviors. Your teacher will help you with presentation

of the speech throughout the course through feedback about your delivery and suggestions. There is also a brief section in Appendix D that provides some general information about speech delivery.

▪ Public Speaking and Decision Making

The approach to this class is based on the belief that **speech preparation and presentation is a series of decisions made by the speaker**. The end result of a series of decisions made by the speaker is a public speech. For example, the speaker deliberately decides in the speech preparation stage what topic to speak about, how to organize the speech, and what to wear when presenting the speech. In addition, when the speaker is actually in front of the audience delivering the speech, decisions such as increasing volume are usually deliberate. An illustration of how the series of decisions speakers need to make work together to create a speech is found on page 9.

Global and Local Decisions

This course will focus on decisions of speech building. Think of the speech preparation decisions a speech builder makes as belonging in two categories: **Global Decisions**, those decisions that have an impact on the whole speech or at least a major portion of it; and **Local Decisions**, decisions that are exclusive to one section of the speech. Examples of Global Decisions include: the choices of topic, overall goal of speech (desired audience impact), thesis and main points, and pattern of organization. Local Decisions are those choices the speaker makes about specific content within major divisions of the speech: whether to begin the introduction with a story or a question, whether to use statistical or expert opinion support to develop a supporting claim, and what words to use in the final appeal in the conclusion.

Communicators make choices when they plan *any kind* of message. For example, during classroom discussion, you decide whether or not to respond to a teacher's question; you may even briefly practice what you will say and how you will say it. You decide whether to write a letter to a company to complain about a defective product, and you decide to whom you will address the letter, what you want to say, and the words you want to use. In both written composition and speech composition, the creator's choices follow a general order. Some decisions, usually Global Decisions, just have to be made before the composer can go on to other decisions. However, both types of human discourse, written and oral, are subject to revision.

Decision-Making to Create a Speech

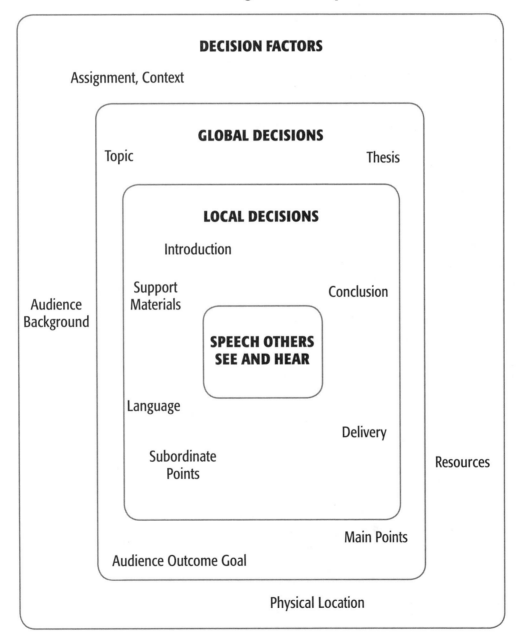

ACTIVITY **1.2**
Observing Decision Areas

Read the following essay about the deliberate decisions Edgar Allen Poe made when creating one of the most familiar English language poems. After you have read the essay, you will be asked to make a list of the specific decisions he made and to decide whether each represents a *global* or *local* decision.

"*A guide for writers, evermore*" by James Kilpatrick

Richard Nixon was a great one for outlines. Whatever the former president's faults may have been—and these were numerous—he was possessed of an orderly mind. Across the terrain of a yellow legal tablet he marched to the cadence of Roman numerals: **I, II, III, IV,** and so to his conclusion. Before he summoned a speechwriter to expand his ideas, Nixon knew exactly where he wanted to go and how he intended to get there.

This is a sound practice for every writer. Whether we are composing a letter, a sermon, a book review, a novel, an editorial or a term paper, we ought to have a clear picture of what we mean to accomplish. Otherwise our train of thought is likely to wander away on sidetracks.

One writer who faithfully observed this rule was Edgar Allan Poe. Not long ago I came across his essay on "The Philosophy of Composition" in which he described exactly how he came to write "The Raven." There are lessons here for all of us. The work, said Poe, "proceeded step by step to its completion, with the precision and rigid consequence of a mathematical problem."

Poe began with a determination to write a poem that would be "not above the popular while not below the critical taste." He held to a theory that "there is a distinct limit, as regards length, to all works of literary art." That is, the work must be capable of being read at a single sitting. He thus set out to write a poem of about 100 lines. "The Raven" he wrote turned out to have 108.

Having settled upon the desired length, Poe then went to the choice of an impression, or tone, to be conveyed. He decided upon a tone of sadness. Of all topics, he asked himself, what is the most melancholy? His answer was "death," and most notably, the death of a beautiful young woman.

His theme is now established. Poe turned next to the mechanics of poetry. He wanted a mournful refrain that could be echoed stanza by stanza.

He wanted a single word containing a sonorous long "o." The word "nevermore" at once presented itself. How was this device to be employed? He turned up the idea of a non-human being. He thought at first of giving the refrain to a parrot, but abandoned the idea in favor of a raven. The ill-omened bird would speak to a lover lamenting his dead mistress.

The plan was complete. It remained only to choose the rhythm in alternating lines of eight feet and seven and a half feet. At last he took pen in hand. And then Poe wrote the last stanzas. The poem "had its beginning at the end, where all works of art should begin." He had his sorrowing student inquire if he ever again "shall clasp a sainted maiden whom the angels name Lenore—clasp a rare and radiant maiden whom the angels name Lenore?" As we all know, quoth the Raven, "nevermore."

The point is that Poe knew where he was going before he set out. Not every writer, to be sure, is as disciplined as Poe, or as tightly organized as Richard Nixon, but the best compositions, regardless of length, share the same dedication to a plan.

To read the sonnets of Shakespeare, or of Elizabeth Barrett Browning, is to form a conviction that they began with their final couplets. The best editorial writers, in my observation, have their concluding cracker in mind before they write the opening sentence. The writers of mystery stories know how effective this can be. Everything leads up to the last page.

Briefly list six decisions Poe made while writing "The Raven."

	Decision	**Global or Local**
1.		
2.		
3.		
4.		
5.		
6.		

▣ Decision Factors

Public speakers do not have total freedom when preparing and presenting a speech. The speech is always shaped by one or more limiting factors. The term **Decision Factors** is used to refer to any significant element that influences the speaker's personal freedom to make decisions about a speech. Even if a speaker is told, "Speak on any topic you wish; talk as long as you wish," the speaker has personal limitations, such as the amount of time available for preparation, or the level of knowledge and understanding the speaker already has or is able to acquire. In most cases there are also external factors, such as audience knowledge and interest in the subject, which the speaker considers when preparing and presenting the speech. We have grouped the decision factors that successful speakers take into consideration as they make the decisions about what to say and how to say it in their speeches. The *four* categories of *Decision Factors* are (a) Assignment and Context Factors, (b) Audience Background Factors, (c) Resource Factors, and (d) Physical Location.

Before speakers make either Global or Local Decisions, it is wise to collect information about Decision Factors and begin to weigh the impact of their findings on speech preparation and presentation decisions. Decision factors continue to influence the speech builder throughout the process of speech construction and presentation. Speakers (a) make tentative decisions, (b) check their decisions against the requirements and limitations imposed by decision factors, (c) revise their decisions, and (d) recheck their decisions. This recursive exercise of plan, check, revise, recheck is often carried out almost intuitively and automatically. The discussion in the next chapter may help you enlarge your awareness of important decision factors and practice a more extensive checking procedure during speech planning.

ACTIVITY **1.3**
Applying Terms and Concepts

The terms **Decision Factors**, **Global Decisions**, and **Local Decisions** may be applied to any situation where a person must make a series of decisions to carry out a process. To give you more practice using the terms, complete the following example:

You are planning a dinner for four friends. The following statements refer to your dinner plans. Write the appropriate label for each statement.

1. Will serve fortune cookies at the end of the meal.   _____

2. Cook only knows how to make four meals:

    (a) pancakes and sausage

    (b) grilled steak and baked potatoes

    (c) Mexican dinner

    (d) Chinese dinner   _____

3. Will use chopsticks.   _____

4. Will prepare Chinese dinner.   _____

5. Has a budget of no more than $4 per guest.   _____

6. Will prepare two meat/fish and vegetable dishes and rice.   _____

7. Cannot begin to *cook* until 30 minutes before guests arrive.   _____

8. One dish will have shrimp in it.   _____

9. Will prepare the vegetables for shrimp dish the night before and store in plastic bag in refrigerator.   _____

ACTIVITY **1.4**
Illustrating Terms and Concepts

Create an ***illustration on paper*** of *Decision Factors*, *Global Decisions*, and *Local Decisions*, their subdivisions, and **how the three relate to each other.** This may be in the form of a chart or graph, but you must do more than just use words. You may draw, paint, use cutouts, or any other techniques. This is an opportunity to express your graphic creativity while solidifying your understanding of the terms and concepts of speech planning.

■ Key Concepts

Listed below are some key concepts from this chapter. Test yourself by seeing if you can explain and give examples of each.

- process of speech preparation

- global decisions

- local decisions

- decision factors

Chapter Study Guide
You should be able to:
• Summarize the overall plan of the course.
• Explain the speech preparation process as a series of decisions.
• Define and differentiate among the terms: *Decision Factors, Global Decisions, Local Decisions.*
• Illustrate the relationship of *Decision Factors, Global Decisions,* and *Local Decisions* either graphically or through an example.

CHAPTER 2
Decision Factors

Chapter Objectives
After reading the chapter you should be able to:
• Identify and analyze Assignment and Context Factors that influence a speech.
• Explain and be able to use either an Indirect or Direct Approach to collect information about Audience Background.
• Analyze availability and impact of Resources from both speaker and outside that influence speech.
• Identify and analyze elements from the Physical Location that influence a speech.

Assignment and Context Factors

Whether you are preparing a speech for this class or for a work or social situation, you will probably be given some guidelines about the type and length of speech you are to present. In addition to the explicit assignment instructions, there are informal expectations related to the speaking situation or context that will affect the speaker's decisions. This section considers three categories of **Assignment and Context Factors**: (1) Speech Goals, (2) Time Limitations, and (3) Expectations and Conventions.

Speech Goals

With one exception, the speech assignments for this class allow the speaker the flexibility to choose the impact the speaker plans and hopes to achieve with respect to the audience. The one exception, the argument speech, requires the speaker to plan a speech consistent with a persuasive speech goal. In the professional and social world outside the classroom, a company or organization representative may predetermine the goal of a speech. For example, speakers may be asked to teach a skill, to report on an issue, or to convince an audience to accept a new policy.

The first two examples of audience outcomes fall under one of the traditional informative categories for outcomes or purposes of speeches—*the audience will gain information and/or understanding*. The third example represents one of the traditional persuasive categories—*the audience will be convinced to change their beliefs and/or be motivated to take action*. Other well-accepted speech outcome groupings include: *the audience will be entertained* and *the audience will be inspired*.

As you listen to speeches and prepare speeches, you may discover that many speeches result in more than one audience outcome. You may find yourself laughing all through a lecture in a sociology class and also come away from that experience realizing that you have gained a great deal of new knowledge. Before an audience can be persuaded to support a bond issue to build a new school, they must be informed of what strategies the school board employed in the past to stretch their resources to meet the need for more classroom space. As a speech builder in this class, you need not be overly concerned if you include elements that produce more that one outcome (entertainment, information acquisition, persuasion) within one speech. However, the predominant mood, content, and strategies should work together to produce one primary outcome.

Time Limitations

Another requirement you will have to consider for each assignment is *minimum* and *maximum time limitations*. For some students, this factor creates difficulty since they already have in mind what they wish to say in the speech, and feel everything they have read and heard on the topic is important. These students frequently have trouble staying under the maximum time limit. Audiences usually find speeches more interesting and are able to remember more of the speech if the speaker has first edited the speech to contain only those elements truly necessary to produce the intended outcome. Other speakers simply want to get back to the safety of their own seat as soon as possible and plan such a short speech that they do not really fulfill the specific elements of the assignment nor give their audience an adequate treatment of the topic.

Speakers also have time boundaries in most speaking situations outside the classroom. Students actively signal to a professor who is going past the class time limit by gathering up belongings and putting on their coats; ministers plan a sermon each week of approximately the same length that neatly fits the same niche in the order of the church service; the guest speaker at the Rotary Club must limit speaking time because the members need to finish their lunches and leave. Speakers for special lectures are usually given time limits by the hosts, or the speakers ask how long they are expected to speak. Convention presentations are strictly monitored for time so that the sessions can stay on schedule. By developing the habit of self-monitoring speech length while preparing and presenting speeches during this class, you will be perceived as a courteous, competent speaker as you easily follow time limit guidelines in other settings as well.

Expectations and Conventions of Audiences, Organizations, or Teacher

Listeners will come to a speech with certain expectations. If a speaker speaks to the same group frequently, for example your public speaking class, the conventions (unwritten rules) will be discovered for speakers in that situation. It will be discovered, for example, whether the teacher strictly enforces the time limits or gives thirty-seconds leeway; whether classmates get embarrassed and giggle when a speaker talks about safe sex or they perceive the topic of safe sex to be such a serious subject that they quietly concentrate on the speaker's message. It is very difficult to discover all the preferences of an audience even if the speaker has spoken before the group frequently. The best approach is to pay careful attention to class members' reactions during both your speeches and other students' speeches. Written and oral feedback, from the teacher and your peers, will give you additional information about what is expected of a speaker in this setting.

Audiences are more apt to consider the speech and speaker as successful if what they see and hear fits their preconceptions of what a speech on this occasion should be. Nevertheless, too much emphasis on audience pleasing can work against the speaker. Since the students in this class are studying the art and craft of public speaking, their expectations and mental images of a "successful" speech will probably undergo constant change during the term. As listeners learn more about speechmaking techniques, they may no longer be satisfied with an amusing ramble about "Lines I Use to Pick Up Dates in Bars," but will expect a well-structured speech dealing with a current national topic such as "Term Limits for Elected Representatives."

There is a danger that a speaker may focus too much on the expectations of the audience. While adapting to what the audience wants to hear and see is beneficial, the speaker will pay a price for denying his or her own beliefs and values. An audience will spot insincerity and respond negatively to the speaker. A speaker can use knowledge of expectations and conventions and still avoid pandering to an audience just to get a favorable reaction.

■ Audience Background Factors

In addition to audiences' general expectations about what speakers and speeches should be like, audience members bring their own specific backgrounds related to the specific topic of the speech. Each audience member's background influences three listener characteristics that are important to speech planning: (1) *listener knowledge*, (2) *listener interest*, and (3) *listener attitudes*.

Listener Knowledge

When planning a speech, it is essential that the speaker discover the audience members' level of prior knowledge about the topic so the speaker can make choices that result in a speech that is neither too difficult for nor too familiar to the audience.

Listener Interest

Influencing the speaker's choices will also be the level of interest the audience has in the topic before the speech. Many people are intrigued by unexplained phenomenon, or the lives of the rich and famous. Just notice how many people covertly scan *The National Enquirer* at the supermarket check-out counter), but may not automatically lean forward to listen when the speaker announces that today's speech will inform them how to balance their checkbooks. In this case, the speaker's awareness of the lack of inherent interest will guide the speaker in creating a "need to know" in the minds of the audience to gain and maintain their interest.

Listener Attitudes

A third category of audience background that influences speech building decisions is that of audience members' attitudes. On controversial issues, listeners may strongly support the speaker's stand, or ardently fight against the speaker's viewpoint, or even feel apathetic about the whole topic. Awareness of the opinions, beliefs, and values of as many of the audience members as possible can guide speakers as they decide what to say, how much to say, and what order to say it in.

How do speakers go about obtaining information about audience knowledge, interest, and attitudes? There are two general approaches to analyzing the background of audience members; (1) The Indirect Approach, and (2) The Direct Approach.

The Indirect Approach

The indirect approach relies on collecting general information about the audience by noting demographic characteristics and using the data to induce general statements about audience knowledge, interests, and beliefs. **Demographic features** refer to obvious individual characteristics that allow the observer to place audience members in categories by those features. For example, age, gender, educational level, economic status, political affiliation, and geographical location are all demographic characteristics. At the end of this section, you will find a sheet on which to record demographic information about your public speaking section. Notice that some characteristics are those listed above; others are demographic factors that are specific to the college population such as year in college and major.

For this class, your teacher may ask you to use the sheet (page 25) to formally create a demographic summary of your classroom audience. For speeches outside the classroom, you may be able, before preparing your speech, to deliberately collect data about the makeup of your audience. In other cases, you may just informally scan the audience and mentally record the ratio of men to women, the ages of audience members, and your guesses about educational level or work background. Some speakers actually carry out an informal demographic survey while giving the speech. Early in the speech, the speaker might ask audience members to put up their hands to respond to such questions as where they are from or if they have had a course that covered the same topic as the speech.

Once the speaker, either formally or informally, has created a demographic analysis of the audience, then the speaker can use the data to extrapolate conclusions from the data about audience background as it relates to the speaker's topic. Educated guesses can be made about the audience level of knowledge by looking at patterns of factors such as educational level, age, work background, and major. Interest levels may be related to these same factors, but the relationship is more tentative, For some topics, gender and affiliation with certain organizations may also be interest predictors. As far as attitudes are concerned, the relationship between which demographic categories are represented and the beliefs of each audience member is very uncertain. As you well know, just being in a particular age category does not mean that everyone in that age group will automatically support a policy such as government-sponsored universal health care. Some college-age students are highly supportive of such a plan; others vigorously oppose it; and still others are completely disinterested in the issue.

The Direct Approach

You can make some assumptions to guide you in your speech-building decisions about the knowledge, interest, and attitudes of your classmates based on the demographic index of the class. However, do not assume all audience members are alike or even that just because you and your classmates have many demographic factors in common, (after all, you are all college students at the same institution in the same speech section) that class members will be similar to you in knowledge, interest, or beliefs. To get more dependable information about audience background, you may need to use the more direct technique of asking your audience survey questions directly related to your topic.

For all classroom speeches, it is helpful to know if your audience is (1) already interested in the topic, (2) how much background information the audience members have on the topic, and (3) how they feel about the topic or related issues before they hear the speech.

Here are some guidelines that will assist you in discovering this information about your audience:

Some Guidelines for Creating Survey Questions

*   If questions cannot *be* answered by a show of hands, speakers will need to provide questions *on* paper for student answers.

*   Yes/No questions are fine if they provide real information. Questions such as "are you interested in topic X?" are not helpful. Most everyone is polite and will say "yes." Likewise, "do you know anything about topic X?" is meaningless because everyone knows something. Yes/No questions such as "Have you ever had a photography class?" provide useful information about how much an audience knows and their level of interest.

*   For the questions where a Yes/No answer alone won't work, provide the opportunity to respond on a continuum. "Not Interested at All; Somewhat Interested; Moderately Interested; Very Interested; Extremely Interested" *or* "Nothing; A Little Bit; A Moderate Amount; A Great Deal; Expert Level" are two sets of potential points on a response continuum.

Ask your teacher if you can hand out written survey questions or have a couple of minutes at the beginning or end of class to survey your class.

ACTIVITY **2.1**
Demographic Information for Public Speaking Class

General Background Survey

1. Age: _____

2. Gender: Female _____ Male _____

3. Year in College: _____

4. College: _____

5. Major: _____

6. Will you be the first family member to graduate from college? Yes _____ No _____

7. Which of the following best describes the location of the home you grew up in?

   City _____ Suburb _____ Medium-Sized Town _____ Small Town _____ Rural _____

8. Which best describes your religious background?

   Catholic _____ Protestant _____ Non-denominational _____ Other _____ None _____

9. Which best describes your political inclinations?

   Democrat _____ Republican _____ Independent _____ Other _____ None _____

10. Is Kansas your home state? (or: What is your home state?) Yes _____ No _____

11. Which best describes where you live during the school year?

    Dorm _____ Greek House _____ Scholarship House _____ Apartment _____
    With Family _____ Other _____

12.

13.

Results

1. Age: Between 15 and 17 _____   Between 18 and 19 _____

   Between 20 and 21 _____   Between 22 and 30 _____   Over 31 _____

2. Gender: Female _____   Male _____

3. Year in College:

   Freshman _____ Sophomore _____ Junior _____ Senior _____ Graduate Student _____

4. College: Arts and Sciences _____ Business _____ Engineering _____ Architecture _____

   Agriculture _____ Human Ecology _____ Education _____

5. Number of different majors: _____ Most common major: _____

6. First Family Graduate: Yes _____ No _____

7. Home Location:

   City _____ Suburb _____ Medium-Sized Town _____ Small Town _____ Rural _____

8. Religion: Catholic _____ Protestant _____ Non-denominational _____ Other _____ None

9. Politics: Democrat _____ Republican _____ Independent _____ Other _____ None _____

10. Home state Kansas: Yes _____ No _____ Other _____

11. School year location:

    Dorm _____ Greek House _____ Scholarship House _____ Apartment _____

    With Family _____ Other _____

12.

13.

Resources

Speakers sometimes find their choices significantly limited by available resources. The boundaries of the possibilities of what a speaker can do may be circumscribed by (1) limited speaker resources, (2) limited external resources, or (3) both.

Speaker Resources

A deliberate analysis of how much the speaker already knows about the topic and how much additional research must be done will help a student decide if an appealing topic is a practical or even possible choice. For example, when only a small amount of preparation time is available, a speaker may be forced to select a more modest plan for visual aids than could be adopted if several months were available to prepare the speech.

As you gain experience, you will be better able to judge what your time, talent, and previous knowledge will allow you to do and do well when preparing a speech. Beginning speakers sometimes equate quantity with quality. They believe that if they try to learn everything about a topic and share their total knowledge base on that subject with their audience, they will surely produce a successful speech. The reality is they frequently run out of preparation time, are not able to master all of the new information, and stumble through a not-ready-for-performance speech.

Outside Resources

Even when speech builders have accurately assessed personal resources and planned accordingly, they may find themselves blocked by limited outside resources. There is a familiar dream that begins with a simple plan to stop by the library and pick up a few books and magazine articles during a thirty-minute block of time. The experience turns into a nightmare when the dreamers find they don't really know how to access the library's computer system, *and* all the books on the subject are missing from the stacks, *and* the periodical articles have to be picked up at a branch library a

mile away. This scenario is a reminder of how the availability, or lack thereof, of outside resources can determine what the speaker is able to do when preparing a speech. All too often the ideal set of pictures, or model, or interview source is not in the same city where the speech student is located and the student will not be able to return home to bring back the perfect speech aid until after the date for presenting the speech.

The lesson here is that making a survey of what outside resources the speaker will need, what the student must do or know to tap into those resources, and what other sources might be substituted can give the student time and opportunity to find appropriate outside resources or to alter the plan of the speech to one that fits within the limitations of outside resources.

Physical Location

The room, furniture, and placement of furniture have an important impact on several of the decisions related to delivering the speech. The use of visual aids in particular depends on such room factors as (a) size, (b) line of sight, and (c) levels of light and darkness in the room. In some cases, a speaker may realize that small models, or even posters, cannot be seen effortlessly by the entire audience; consequently some type of projection system must be chosen if the audience is to benefit from the visual illustrations. The speaker must also be located where he or she can easily be seen and heard by the audience. This may necessitate moving some of the furniture, including where audience members will sit. Speaker visibility and audibility, on the other hand, may be achieved simply by the speaker moving closer to the audience, or deciding to remove a massive speaker's stand that hides all but the upper face of the speaker.

Although physical location has less influence on content aspects of the speech such as topic, organization, and support materials, there are some cases where the speaker has to make speech content adjustments because of location factors. It is certainly more difficult to speak on a sensitive personal topic in a field house before a massive audience than in a small room with twenty listeners seated in a circle. Recognizing the increased difficulty of connecting with individuals in a large audience with barriers of space and size gives the speaker an opportunity to consider adaptive strategies when making content choices.

Another aspect of physical location may require both content and delivery changes. This occurs when the speaker realizes that certain elements of the physical environment will or are making the audience members uncomfortable or inattentive. When the temperature of the room is too high or too low, the room is stuffy or bombarded by outside noise or glaring light, or the audience members are hungry or tired, either the physical factors must be changed or new strategies inserted to help the audience attend to the speech. Planned or spontaneous breaks may be enough to help the audience become engaged in the speech again.

A speaker should, whenever possible, visit the physical location of the speech before the scheduled time of the speech so that necessary changes may be made ahead of time. If it is not possible to adjust the physical surroundings, at least the speaker will then be aware of what needs to be done to ensure the audience members can see, hear, and attend to the speech. When a speaker is already keyed up about speaking to a group, the last distraction that person needs is to suddenly discover there are problems with the physical surroundings that mean either the message cannot get to the audience as planned or the speaker will have to come up with some last-minute improvisations.

Conclusion

The first step in speech construction is to explore the Decision Factors that will guide or at least impose limits on the speech builder's decisions. It is your responsibility to discover as much as you can about the speech and speaking situations before you actively start to research and plan the speech. *Ask questions.*

Be sure you have answers to the following questions.

I.   What are the assignment's characteristics?

    A.   Does the assignment require that I choose a specific type of audience outcome goal or type of speech based on audience outcome? If so, what are the defining characteristics of that outcome?

    B.   Is there a time limit? Will it be rigidly enforced?

    C.   What expectations does the audience or organization or teacher have about me as a speaker? What expectations do they have about the assignment? What expectations do they have about the topic?

    D.   If this is a classroom speech, what are the criteria the speech will be graded on?

II. What is the background of the audience members in regard to my topic as defined in the speech thesis?

    A.   What previous knowledge does the audience have about the topic?

    B.   What is the level of interest the audience has in the topic?

    C.   What is the attitude of the audience toward this topic?

    D.   Why does the audience "need" to hear a speech on this topic?

III. What resources are available for preparing the speech?

    A.   What limits will my time, skills, knowledge, and talent impose on preparing and presenting this speech?

    B.   What special skills, knowledge, talents, and resource contacts do I have that can be used for this speech?

    C.   What limits will outside research resources impose on preparing this speech?

    D.   What appropriate and/or unique outside research resources are available?

    E.   What limits will outside resources for preparing or acquiring visual aids impose on preparing this speech?

    F.   What appropriate and/or unique outside resources for preparing or acquiring visual aids are available?

IV. What are the characteristics of the physical setting where the speech will be presented?

    A. Will the audience be able to effortlessly see and hear me?

    B. Will I be able to rearrange the furniture in the room?

    C. Will a microphone be available if needed?

    D. Are there expected distractions in the environment that I need to consider?

    E. What equipment for presenting visual aids is available? (easel to hold posters or place to tape or tack posters? slide projector? opaque projector? overhead projector? screen? PowerPoint equipment? location of electrical outlets?)

    F. Will the audience have a clear view of visual aids?

Key Concepts

Listed below are some key concepts from this chapter. Test yourself by seeing if you can explain and give examples of each.

- speech goals

- expectations and conventions

- listener characteristics

- indirect approach for analysis

- demographic features

- direct approach for analysis

- speaker resources

- outside resources

- elements of physical location

Chapter Study Guide
You should be able to:
• List and explain impacts of the three decision factor categories under *Assignment and Context Factors.*
• List the three target areas from Audience Background about which speakers need to collect information.
• Explain the *Indirect Approach* of using demographic factors to collect information and *Audience Background.*
• List and explain how four *Demographic Factors* impact on *Audience Interest, Knowledge,* and/or *Attitude.*
• Explain the Direct Approach of using survey questions to collect information about *Audience Background.*
• List guidelines for creating survey questions.
• List and explain impacts of two *Decision Factor* categories under *Resources.*
• Explain impacts of *Physical Location.*

CHAPTER 3
Global and Local Decisions

Chapter Objectives
After reading the chapter you should be able to:
• Identify and apply strategies for finding and choosing Speech Topics.
• Choose and write goals for a speech that reflect how a speech will change audience members Cognitively, Affectively and Behaviorally.
• Choose and write Thesis Statements for planning speeches and Thesis Statements to be shared with an audience.
• Choose and write Main Points that evolve from the thesis.
• Create Subordinate Points to support main points.
• Identify types of Support Materials.
• Determine what behaviors constitute Plagiarism.
• Determine what behaviors constitute Legal/Ethical Violations.

Global Decisions

After the speaker has surveyed the Decision Factors, the next step is to begin to make tentative Global Decisions. These major decisions about the content and form of the speech will affect the whole speech, or at least large blocks of the speech. Global Decisions include (1) selecting the **Speech Topic**, (2) identifing the **Primary Speech Goal**, (3) creating the **Thesis**, and (4) discovering the subdivisions of the thesis, or the **Main Points**. As you read this chapter, it may be helpful to refer to the corresponding diagram.

Global Decisions

```
         Speech topic
              ↓
  Speech Audience Outcome Goals
            ↓ ↑
           Thesis
         ↙  ↓↑  ↘
Main Point 1  Main Point 2  Main Point 3
```

Topic Selection

For most speech occasions beyond the classroom, speakers are selected because they are experts on a specific subject. A member of a club is asked to share his experiences (and slides) from the trip he took to the Middle East. A scholar whose research focuses on birds of the Antarctic speaks (and shows her slides) to the local Audubon club. An employee who has worked in the company's production facility for ten years presents a proposal to a group of managers for reorganizing the traffic patterns within the plant. These speakers already know their general topics for their speeches, but they still must select the specific focus or emphasis of the presentation. Should the speaker try to present an overall picture of the trip or concentrate on a few locations, the people, the architecture, the natural features of the landscape, or the political changes, or what?

Students in public speaking classes usually have a double task: (1) coming up with a subject area for a speech, and (2) narrowing that subject to a speech topic that will fit within the limitations of the Decision Factors. Many students hit a road block before they even start to prepare a speech because they cannot find a speech topic in which they (a) have interest and/or knowledge, (b) believe the audience will have interest, and (c) feel is manageable within the time limit for preparing the speech. Part of the frustration related to finding a speech topic may be due to placing too much emphasis on guessing what the audience would like to hear rather than on what the speaker would like to share and topics about which the speaker already has some prior knowledge.

Begin with what you know. You already know a great deal about many subjects. To create a list of unique areas of experience and knowledge, you can draw on subjects learned through (a) job experiences, (b) courses for an academic major, (c) the mass media (by extensive reading, watching, or listening to information or presentations on a subject), (d) participating in a club, hobby, or any other free choice activity, (e) personal or family travel, or (f) special interest courses.

Try this short exercise. Based on your individual experiences from work, school, family and personal life, write down at least three subject areas which you believe you know more about than most people in the class.

1. _____

_____

2. _____

_____

3. _____

_____

Simply having knowledge about a subject is not a sufficient reason to give a speech on that topic. You may no longer be especially interested in the subject. Playing "Dungeons and Dragons" may have been an all consuming passion five years ago and you may know more about the game than anyone in the known universe, but if you are bored with even thinking about the subject or if you cannot determine why your audience should hear about the game, then discard this as the topic for a speech. Our interest in and dedication to a subject are essential since, as speakers, we will be spending time with that topic and an audience will not be interested in a speech if speakers are not excited about sharing their enthusiasm and inside knowledge about the subject with the listeners.

ACTIVITY **3.1**
Topic Brainstorming

To aid you in finding speech topics throughout the semester, it is useful to create a list of potential speech topics through the technique of brainstorming. Under the four general headings below, write down, without judging or thinking too deeply, as many possible speech topics for yourself as you can come up with. You should include both topics that you already have a great deal of information about or topics that are fairly new to you but you would be interested in learning about and developing the topic.

Work/Vocation/Major	Hobbies/Trips/Leisure Activities
1.	1.
2.	2.
3.	3.
4.	4.
5.	5.
6.	6.
7.	7.
8.	8.
9.	9.
10.	10.

Current Events/Issues	Previous Knowledge/Expertise
1.	1.
2.	2.
3.	3.
4.	4.
5.	5.
6.	6.
7.	7.
8.	8.
9.	9.
10.	10.

The speech topic must also, of course, fit the audience. Try to discover if the audience has a "need to know" about the topic. Obviously, college students do not need to hear a speech that gives the guideline for how to apply to, and be accepted into, an undergraduate college. You may find that you would really like to share your special expertise on a topic such as how to identify the age and quality of antique bottles with your classmates. You love this hobby; you really know a lot about it; but since you are speaking to a general audience of students who have never encountered an antique bottle, you may decide this topic will not work since there is not an obvious "need to know" element relating the topic to the audience. If a topic seems to be "just right" for you as a speaker, instead of discarding the idea, you may be able to create the "need to know." Everyone needs activities to fill free time and relieve stress; bottle collecting can be profitable as an investment; a collector learns about the history of an area and the people through the bottles they have discarded; observing the colors and designs of bottles is an aesthetic experience; bottle making is an example of technological development in mass production. Some of these motivations for hearing a speech on antique bottles do not include an immediate practical application of what the listener will learn during the speech, but simply increase the listener's fund of knowledge.

Don't assume that all knowledge has equal value for all audiences. If several good reasons cannot be found to support how your speech content will enrich the lives of your audience, then perhaps you need to look for a different topic or a different focus on the subject. In the example of a speech on antique bottles, rather than teaching the audience exactly how to date a bottle, the speaker may decide to focus on what can be discovered about the lives of people in the 19th century based on the kinds of bottle found in trash heaps, since this approach intersects with a "need to know" for more audience members.

Students who are sharing information about sports may need to focus on what a spectator or beginner "needs to know" rather than giving specific instructions about exactly how to make an advanced move or carry out a complicated strategy. This same advice applies to speeches that teach the audience how to do or make something. If the speaker does want to concentrate on advanced information or procedures, then instead of teaching the audience the exact steps, the speaker could decide on a focus that will give the audience a general understanding or appreciation of the complexity and sophistication of the subject.

■ Speech Goals for Audience Outcomes

As we have discussed topic selection, we have constantly referred to the audience's needs and the appropriateness of the topic for the audience. The attention that must be paid to the audience when choosing and refining the speech subject illustrates that decision-making for speech building cannot always proceed in a rigid, set order. Decision areas are interconnected, and each decision may influence the choices you make in all other decision categories. The result is that you may make tentative decisions that you then have to amend or even change, or you may simultaneously make several decisions. Probably the decision area which has the most influence over the narrowing of the speech topic is the category of *Primary Speech Goal.*

As discussed earlier, a classroom assignment or the sponsors of your speech may have already set the dominant goal of the speech. You may be told to prepare an "informative speech" or an unbiased report for a class or job assignment. Even when you are not assigned a specific "type" of speech goal, the physical setting and topic make it clear what the speech goal should be. For example, you recognize that your goal is persuasive when you are chosen as the representative speaking to the City Council in favor of the new curbside recycling program.

When the speech goal is left entirely to your discretion, it is still a good idea to deliberately choose a dominant outcome so the audience is not confused by a mixed message. In addition to the Primary Speech Goal, the speaker may have one or more *Secondary Speech Goals*. However, the speech should be planned and executed around one major goal so both the speaker and audience are well aware of the most important mood and outcome. You may have had the experience of leaving a presentation not knowing whether the speaker meant for you to take his or her remarks seriously, or if the remarks were designed just to entertain, or even to persuade through the use of humor.

If the speaker does not start out knowing what he or she wants the audience to experience, the speech may end up as a fragmented cut-and-paste job that baffles the audience and loses credibility for the speaker. Audiences may also react negatively if through most of the speech the speaker appears to be simply sharing unbiased information with them, but at the last minute makes an appeal that obviously is a pitch to buy some product or adopt some policy. Decide on your major outcome and then build a speech that consistently moves toward that goal.

This cautionary advice about focusing on one primary speech goal should not be taken to mean that your speech must rigidly conform to a pattern of only persuasive content or only entertaining messages. Most persuasive speeches depend heavily on the sharing of information. A humorous speech may have a subtle persuasive intent. The key is in knowing where you want to go with the speech and to resolve not to deliberately mislead your audience by appearing to promote an outcome that is contrary to your announced intent. Most audiences will be more receptive to an honest sharing of your chosen purpose for the speech.

The most common Primary Speech Goals are those that focus on one of the following: (a) persuading, (b) informing, (c) entertaining, (d) celebrating, or (e) honoring a person or event. Your Primary and Secondary Speech Goals will serve as the basis for a written **Audience Outcome Goal Statement**. The Audience Outcome Goal Statement is written by speakers to serve as a guide throughout the speech construction phase. Instead of emphasizing a goal naming what the speaker will *do*, such as "inform" or "persuade," the audience outcome goal statement is written from the perspective of *how audience members will be changed as a result of having experienced a speech*. Audience changes fit under three categories: (1) cognitive changes, (2) affective changes, and (3) behavioral changes.

Cognitive changes are changes that occur in what we call the mind. In all probability, most of the speeches you prepare for class will have a cognitive audience change as the dominant audience outcome. The speaker has set cognitive goals when he or she plans that audience members will (a) learn something new, (b) acquire new understanding, (c) change a previously held belief or (d) acquire a new belief. As you can see, cognitive changes may be desired either when the speaker plans to inform (audience learns or understands) or when the speaker hopes to persuade (change a belief).

Affective changes are emotional or attitudinal changes. Affective changes, such as emotional reactions or positive-negative feelings, are often used to further the Primary Audience Outcome and may be stated as Secondary Audience Outcome Goals by the speaker. For instance, a speaker might have a Primary Audience Outcome Goal of trying to change the audience's beliefs toward increasing state sales taxes. This is a cognitive change. To aid in reaching this goal, the speaker might choose the strategy of making the audience feel guilty about having sufficient financial resources when others in the state are suffering and deprived because there are not sufficient state funds to provide for their needs. The goal to create the guilty feeling is a Secondary Audience Outcome Goal that promotes an affective change.

Although it is most common for an affective change to be secondary, the affective response may be the Primary Audience Outcome Goal when speeches are planned with the purpose of entertaining an audience (banquet speech, stand-up comedy routine) or with the purpose of praising or celebrating a person or event. For these special occasions, the speakers hope the audience will have strong emotional experiences throughout the speech.

Behavior changes result in the listeners' actual changes in behavior or actions. Behavioral changes may be either the dominant goal or a secondary goal of the speaker. The planned dominant outcome of many persuasive speeches is to convince the audience to take a specific action. In those cases, the Primary Audience Outcome Goal calling for a behavioral change may be supported by the audience first undergoing a cognitive or affective change (Secondary Audience Outcome Goal) which eventually leads to the altered behavior of audience members. People first have to believe an action is right, justified, or rewarding before they will act. People are more apt to take an action if they feel anger, guilt, love, or desire. Conversely, behavioral changes are Secondary Audience Outcomes when a cognitive change makes the behavior possible, but the speaker has decided his or her central job is to teach the audience the behavior rather than persuade the audience to adopt the behavior.

When planning a speech, the speaker states the Primary Audience Outcome Goal and all relevant Secondary Audience Outcome Goal. In the following examples of Audience Outcome Goal statements, the speaker begins the Primary Outcome Statement with the words "I want my audience to_____."

1. I want my audience to *learn* the steps for baking yeast bread. (Cognitive Change)

2. I want my audience to *believe (or be persuaded)* that following a low-fat diet is essential for good health. (Cognitive Change)

3. I want my audience to be *entertained* by my stories of "how l fell in love with the magic of credit cards." (Affective Change)

Secondary Audience Outcome Goals may be written as a continuation of the Primary Goal Statement or written separately. In the examples below, the Secondary and Primary Goals are in one sentence. Notice that the italicized section of the statement represents the Secondary Audience Outcome Goal. Recognizing that there is more than one goal while stating both goals together helps the speaker become aware of how Secondary Goals working with the Primary Goals influence later Global and Local Decisions.

1. I want my audience to learn the steps for baking yeast breads *so they will be able to bake their own bread.* (a Behavioral Change)

2. I want my audience to believe that following a low-fat diet is essential for good health *so they will begin eating a low-fat diet.* (a Behavioral Change)

3. I want my audience to be entertained by my stories of "how I fell in love with the magic of credit cards" so they will start to realize that it is very easy to abuse credit. (An Affective and Cognitive Change)

Notice that the choice the speaker makes for the application of the information in example 1 will influence how the speaker develops that speech. Since the speaker has the goal of the audience learning the skill and art of bread baking at a level where the audience can actually replicate the process, then the speaker must plan to build into the speech clear, *complete* instructions that the audience totally understands *and* will *remember.* In preparing this speech, the author must deliberately plan to model each unfamiliar step of the process and use repetition and written instructions to help the audience remember what ingredients are needed and how to combine them.

Instead of the goals listed in the previous example, suppose the speaker chooses the following audience outcome: I want my audience to learn the steps for baking yeast breads so they will appreciate the investments in time and effort pioneer homemakers had to spend on baking bread for their families. For this speech, the audience members will not need to remember each detail of what goes into the bread or have a total comprehension of how to scald milk, dissolve yeast, or knead the dough. The first audience outcome almost demands demonstration and extensive visual aids. The second might depend more on example, statistics, and even narration in addition to listing and explaining the steps.

This second approach to the bread-baking speech is an example of audience application of "knowledge for its own sake" or simply an increase in the audience's fund of information. *What* the audience will do with the information does not always have to be a practical application.

ACTIVITY **3.2**
Audience Outcome Goal Statements

For the second and third examples of Audience Outcome Goal statements given previously, rewrite the second part of the statement in such a way that "what the audience will do" changes the content and strategies used in the speech.

2. I want my audience to believe that following a low-fat diet is essential for good health so they will

_____

_____

3. I want my audience to be entertained by my stories of "how I fell in love with the magic of credit cards" so they will

_____

_____

Now practice writing some Audience Outcome Goal Statements. Use one of the topics you choose earlier in the chapter because of your special expertise. Write two different Audience Outcome Goal Statements for the topic. Be sure to include both Primary and Secondary Goals.

Topic _____

Audience Outcome Statement _____

Audience Outcome Statement _____

Audience Outcome Statement _____

Audience Outcome Statement _____

Thesis

Perhaps the most useful tool in speech planning and presentation is the speech Thesis. The speaker distills the most important ideas of the speech and writes the product of the condensation in one sentence called the **Thesis Statement**. The Thesis Statement will be defined and explained later in this section, hut first we will consider the nature of the Thesis itself.

Nature of the Thesis

The **Thesis** is the central claim of the speech. Claims are the basic units of speech just as cells are considered the basic units of living organisms. **Claims** are general statements that the speaker asserts are true. For example, you meet someone and she *exclaims*, "This is a beautiful day." Or a friend *proclaims*, "I'll never get all my work done." The basic pattern of speech construction is that of (1) making claims, and then (2) supporting the claim. The person who claims it is a beautiful day may go ahead and support the claim by pointing out that the sun is shining, the wind is gentle, and the temperature is warm.

In a similar way, a speaker chooses a central claim called a Thesis and the rest of the speech is created to support that claim. Because a speech is much longer and more complex than the simple statement about a beautiful day, the support of the Thesis is also more extensive and complex. Consequently, in addition to the central claim, the speaker will depend on other claims to develop or support the Thesis. The second level of claims designed to support the Thesis are the **Main Points** of the speech. The main points in turn may be supported by lower level claims called **Subordinate Points**, and finally by **Support Materials**. The concept of claims and support for claims is basic to speech building. You will encounter these ideas not only in relation to the Thesis but throughout the course. In essence, the art and craft of speech building depends on the skills of identifying claims and supporting those claims.

Functions of Thesis

The process of constructing your Audience Outcome Goals Statement has resulted in a specific focus within your general speech topic area. The Thesis will solidify that focus and also provide the organizational plan for developing the subject in the speech. Like the Audience Outcome Goals Statement, the Thesis Statement serves initially to guide the speaker during the construction of the speech.

The Thesis and a preview of Main Points should be shared orally with the audience in the introduction of the speech. The speaker may choose whether to explicitly announce the Audience Outcome Goal Statement to the audience, however, telling the audience exactly what the topic is and how it will be developed is essential for two reasons. First, the audience can mentally participate in the speech as it develops if they know the encircling limits of the topic and the planned order in which that topic will be developed. Including the audience by sharing the planned structure of the speech allows them to listen more efficiently and remain interested. Audience involvement in the speech as it unfolds, based on understanding the speech structure, also helps the audience remember the speech content. It is easier to remember what the speaker said if the audience has a small number of landmarks (the Main Points) on which to hang the detailed information presented in the speech.

Since oral presentations are ephemeral collections of words that appear briefly and disappear, audiences need as much help as possible to capture and retain the speaker's message. Unless the speech has been taped, only the parts that stick in the memory of the audience will remain after a few seconds. In written discourse, the audience can go back and read and reread to participate and re-participate in the author's message. Readers may enjoy searching for the author's plan which has been interwoven in the text and only partly disclosed. Listeners need to have blatant messages of organization so they can capture the plan in order to follow the speech.

The second motive for presenting an obvious plan of speech development is to lead the audience to conclude that the speech is well-organized and that the speaker is highly competent. A speech may actually have a beautifully crafted structure, but the audience may not be able to pick it out while performing the juggling act of listening and watching the complex array of stimuli that occur during the oral presentation. Therefore, in order to remove any doubt about the well-planned structure of your speech, tell your audience just what your subject is and just how you will explore the subject in the speech.

Thesis in Speech Planning

Throughout the process of working on a speech, the creators should have before them a written **Thesis Statement**. A Thesis Statement is a one-sentence encapsulation of the speech. It guides all decisions about what to say in the speech. It may seem difficult to condense a 30-minute speech or even a 10-minute speech into one sentence. Start with a tentative Thesis Statement that includes (1) naming the speech topic as the subject of your sentence and (2) a statement about that topic or your version of that topic as the predicate. Returning to the example of baking bread, you might say, "*The process of baking bread* (the narrowed speech topic as sentence subject) *includes three major steps* (your development of the topic as sentence predicate and, in this case, sentence object). An alternative development of the topic as expressed as a Thesis is: "*The process of baking bread in pioneer days* (a slightly different focus for the same general topic) *was difficult and time-consuming* (a very different development of the topic).

By limiting yourself to one sentence, you enhance the probability that your speech will be cohesive and, because you will avoid extraneous side-trips to topics not included under the one sentence, that the speech will be easily remembered by the audience.

ACTIVITY 3.3
Thesis Statements

To reinforce your understanding of the Thesis, write one-sentence Thesis Statements for the speech topics discussed earlier in the chapter related to low-fat diets and credit cards. Remember the pattern is to first name the narrowed topic as the subject of the sentence and complete the sentence by a statement related to how the topic will be developed, or a statement that describes or defines the topic.

Topic _____

Thesis Statement _____

_____

_____

Topic _____

Thesis Statement _____

_____

_____

Now write two additional examples of Thesis Statements using one or two of your personal speech topics.

Topic _____

Thesis Statement _____

_____

_____

Topic _____

Thesis Statement _____

_____

_____

Thesis Presented Orally In Speech Introduction

When you announce your Thesis to the audience just before you begin the body of the speech, you will be repeating the same essential elements you used in writing a Thesis Statement for planning the speech, but your words will change. The **Planning Thesis** was written for the speaker by the speaker to guide his or her speech building choices, but the **Oral Speech Thesis** is written for the audience to guide them in mentally participating in and following the speech. The most obvious way to express this Thesis to the audience is to signal the audience with a statement such as "Today I will teach you the process of baking bread by showing you the three basic steps." A speaker does not have to exactly follow this model, but it will help the audience most if he uses a direct statement that warns the audience, "Listen. Here comes the Thesis." You may be uncomfortable with a choice that seems like the equivalent of a brass band and flashing lights, but remember, the listening audience only gets one shot to discover what your specific topic is and how you will develop it.

■ Main Points

Relationship of Thesis and Main Points

The **Main Points**, those first level claims that support the Thesis, should logically evolve from the two parts of the Thesis statement. They are the subordinate ideas that are the natural divisions of the Thesis and will be presented as the labels for the major divisions of the body of the speech.

In our first example of the process of baking bread, the three major steps of baking bread become the Main Points. You can see that because the speaker decided to focus on the *process* rather than, for example, the history of baking bread or different types of homemade bread, the speaker has already made a decision that the body of the speech will be divided into the sequential steps of the bread-making process.

At this point in planning the speech, the speaker should look at the Thesis Statement and determine what subtopics logically flow from the claim and what subtopics are not appropriate in the body of the speech, since they are not included within the domain of the Thesis. If the Thesis and the Main Points are *mutually inclusive*, the speech will have coherence and the audience probability of remembering the speech as a whole and its component parts will be greatly enhanced. **Mutual inclusiveness** means that everything included in the Main Points also is included in the Thesis. Envision the Thesis as the circumference of a circle. Everything covered in the Main Points lies within that circle.

Students sometimes violate this principle of mutual inclusiveness when they plan to begin a speech, such as the one on the process of baking bread, by including some information about the history of yeast breads or an explanation of how yeast works to make the dough rise. When the speech is focused on the process of how to make bread, history and yeast digestion are outside the circle of process steps and cannot be used as Main Points. They are related to the topic, but do not support the central claim that includes only the process. This does not mean that the history of bread-making or yeast digestion cannot be included in the speech either as background material in the introduction or under one of the Main Points. However, they do not represent major steps in the process of making bread and, therefore, are not an inherent part of the Thesis Statement and its first-level divisions.

To help solidify the relationship between Thesis and Supporting Claims in your mind, create and briefly explain a *metaphor* that demonstrates the characteristic of mutual inclusiveness. Here are a couple of metaphors to help you get started on an original example.

Example 1

The relationship between the Thesis and Main Points is like an egg. The Thesis is the shell and the Main Points are the yoke and whites. The Main Points are completely included within the shell.

Example 2

The relationship between the Thesis and Main Points is like a family and its members. The label of "Smith family" stands for all the members. It does not include any outsiders such as Billy Jones from next door. Billy fits under the label of "Jones Family." Both are families, but they are different families just as two different Thesis Statements can be created for the same Speech Topic, but only those Main Points that fit under each Thesis can be included in the supporting claims for the central claim.

Metaphor for Mutually Inclusive Thesis and Main Points:

_____

_____

_____

_____

_____

_____

_____

_____

_____

_____

Effective Wording of Main Points

A language strategy to increase interest in the structure of the speech and aid retention of the plan is to select short, repetitive labels for the Main Points. An audience will remember "Prepare the Dough; Work the Dough; Bake the Dough." Some speakers try to find key words that all begin with the same sound or rhyme with each other. A well-known McDonald's campaign stressing "Food, Folks, and Fun" is an example of using language sounds to get attention and promote memory.

Number of Main Points

For a class speech, it is usually suggested that the speech be divided into *two to five* Main Points. If speakers have fewer than two, they obviously don't have division, and if speakers have divided the body into more than five major categories, they probably have used some minor claims. Many speeches have three Main Points, but it is certainly acceptable to have fewer or more. The number is determined by the speech topic. It is important to ensure that all Main Points are equal in importance and approximately equal in the time and space they require to be developed. If some appear to be less significant or can be expressed in under a minute, they are probably not major Main Points and need to be worked into the speech in a subordinate position.

ACTIVITY **3.4**
Main Points

You've already guessed what comes next. Yes, create and write Main Points for the Thesis Statements you developed for the 2nd and 3rd sample topics on low-fat diet and credit cards. You may discover that you have to revise the Thesis Statements in order to create Main Points that are mutually inclusive with the Thesis.

Thesis Statement _____

_____

Main Points _____

_____

Thesis Statement _____

_____

Main Points _____

_____

Now also write two more sets of Main Points using your own topics.

Thesis Statement _____

_____

Main Points _____

_____

Thesis Statement _____

_____

Main Points _____

_____

▪ Local Decisions

Local Decisions control subsections of the speech. Their influence may extend over a significant portion of the speech such as the development of an entire Main Point or they may control as small a fraction of the speech as the pronunciation of one syllable of one word. Local Decisions are all of the elements that flesh-out, clothe, adorn, develop, and support the skeleton of the speech created during the process of making Global Decisions. Local Decisions are those choices that allow speakers to put their own unique stamps of authorship on the speech. These choices largely determine the level of success of the speech as far as audience interest, understanding, and memory of the speech content are concerned. The two categories of Local Decisions that will be covered at this time are: (1) *Subordinate Points* and (2) *Support Materials*. A third category, Introductions and Conclusions, will be discussed in Chapter 7. Local Decisions related to Language and Delivery Behaviors will be covered within other topics and in the Appendix.

Subordinate Points

The term "supporting claims" has been used up to this time primarily to refer to the first level of divisions the speech builder makes when subdividing the Thesis or central claim into the blocks that will become the major sections of the body of the speech. All supporting claims are expressions of *ideas or concepts* and are usually written in rather abstract language.

Some very short speeches may have only the first-level supporting claims called Main Points. When constructing a speech, if you discover that your first-level idea does not logically separate into two or more subordinate ideas, you are probably ready to go ahead and make decisions about the support materials you will use to illustrate, reinforce, or explain the concept. Students who like to use a formal outline structure to graphically plan the body of the speech use Roman Numerals to label first-level Main Points (I., II., III.). More specific information will be listed under these first-level claims, either second-level supporting claims called Subordinate Points or specific support materials such as examples, stories, statistics, quotations, and explanations. This second level in formal outlining is indicated by capital letters (A., B., C.).

To carefully work out the development of a Main Point, speakers often need to go ahead and commit themselves to third- or even fourth-level content, either further subdivision of ideas or the concrete information that will be presented to support the ideas. When the speaker chooses second- and/or third-level claims or concrete support for the claims and records those decisions in an outline or organizational map, the speaker is planning the logical development of the ideas, *not necessarily the order that will be used when orally presenting the content.*

The speaker may choose to begin a section of the speech with a set of very specific facts that have been located at the third-level of the outline or map explaining later that those details illustrate or support the major concept being discussed in that portion of the speech. The general order of decisions when planning the body of the speech is to move from the most general decisions to the most specific-begin with the Thesis Statement, move to the first-level Main Points, then to second- and third-level Subordinate Points and on to Support Materials at lower levels. Remember that graphically representing the speech parts with an outline or map is a *planning* tool, not necessarily a system to be used as speaking notes or to control the order of specific content in the speech.

Support Materials

Support Materials are more concrete and more specific than claim statements and have the function of developing and supporting the claims of the speech. Most of your classtime presentations in this course will be assignments that allow you to prepare and present specific types of Support Materials. By developing a repertoire of Support Materials and using a variety of appropriate support in your longer speeches, you will be able to avoid the weakness of many speeches that result in audience disinterest, audience confusion, and audience inability to remember the speech or its content.

Speakers sometimes make the mistake of trying to support or develop their claims by restating the ideas using alternate wording but continuing to use abstract language. That is exactly what I have done in the previous sentence. As you can tell, that approach does little to clarify or interest the audience. Instead, as often and as quickly as the speaker can, he should move to concrete specific choices such as examples, stories, or comparisons. To help you build your catalogue of Support Materials, this text will discuss some of the most useful categories of Support Materials: (1) Narration, (2) Definition, (3) Description, (4) Comparison, (5) Memorization, (6) Evidence, and (7) Argumentation.

In practice, these categories often overlap; parts of several methods can be used within the development of a claim. However, for purposes of instruction, we will consider each strategy separately. In the actual classroom speech for each Support Material category, you may find you are predominantly presenting the one assigned type of Support Materials, but including elements from other categories. This blending is appropriate, and as long as what you have to say both fulfills the assignment and works to support the claim, you should not be concerned.

Legal, Ethical, and Rhetorical Sensitivity as Related to Speech Content

The Issue of Plagiarism

Students need to have a clear understanding of just what plagiarism is in regard to both global and local decisions. Almost all speeches include some ideas or materials that come from someone else. For concepts and facts so well-known they can be labeled "common knowledge," there is no problem. When a speaker within the speech clearly gives credit to the author for that person's ideas, words, or evidence, again there is no problem. Most students agree, however, that when the exact words of another are used without giving a source, it is implied that those are the speaker's words. Then that person has plagiarized.

However, there are several gray areas about what constitutes plagiarism. Students are often tempted to take well-written sentences, clear organization, or unique approaches from magazine articles, books, or other students' speeches without giving credit to the original thinker or writer. The "borrowing" of another's work is sometimes only a half-conscious action stimulated by admiration for the author's expertise and skill. Plagiarism extends beyond just using someone else's words. It includes using an author's original ideas, examples, and unique plans of organization without sharing the source of those ideas, examples, or organization with the audience.

In cases where a team or pair of students work together, then the speech should be presented as the work of all members who contributed to its creation. If two speakers research and plan their speeches together and then each presents the speech as his or her own independent work, something is not right. It is not the total work of either speaker and should not be presented as such.

Public speakers must not plagiarize. Not only is this "intellectual thievery" a serious ethical offense, but when students use other's work, they cheat themselves of vital first-hand experiences in speech preparation. The speakers' lack of familiarity with organization, ideas, or word choices that they did not generate often will show up in ineffective delivery. Speakers ultimately pay when they skip steps in the speech building process. Finally, students who plagiarize run the risk of serious consequences to their academic careers.

Provisions for dealing with proven cases of plagiarism are usually spelled out in university policy documents. More information about the Honor and Integrity System at Kansas State University can be found at www.k-state.edu/honor.

ACTIVITY 3.5
Plagiarism*

Read the situations given below and by talking with others in the group decide if the student has committed plagiarism. Be able to defend your group's decisions orally.

1. Susan takes an entire speech from a book, memorizes it, and then delivers it in class as if it were her own work.

    Susan (has) (has not) plagiarized.

    Reasons _____

    _____

    _____

2. Kent finds an outline of a speech on the Bermuda Triangle in his fraternity files. He adds one additional example to the speech but otherwise does not change it. Kent then presents the speech in class as his own.

    Kent (has) (has not) plagiarized.

    Reasons _____

    _____

    _____

3. Theresa reads an article from the *Reader's Digest* on the relationship between smoking and heart disease. Since the article first covers the adverse effects of smoking on the circulatory system and then shows how patients' health improves when they stop smoking, Theresa decides to organize her speech in the same way. During her speech she does not mention that she is using the same problem-solution organization as that of the magazine article.

    Theresa (has) (has not) plagiarized.

    Reasons _____

    _____

    _____

---

*   This activity is similar to an activity created by Nancy Goulden and published in the Instructor's Manual for Verderber's "The Challenge of Effective Speaking" published by Wadsworth Publishing Company, 1997.

4. Maria uses statistics extensively in her speech on toxic waste but does not tell where she found the statistics.

   Maria (has) (has not) plagiarized.

   Reasons _____

   _____

   _____

5. Patrice finds an unusual approach to the problem of drinking and driving in a magazine article. The author recommends that there be no age limits on buying or drinking alcohol, but that the legal age for a driver's license be twenty-five years of age. When presenting the speech, Patrice says, "I am supporting a plan described by Jesse Wilson in the May 1997 issue of *Safe Driver*. I will describe Mr. Wilson's proposal and give you my reasons for believing it will work."

   Patrice (has) (has not) plagiarized.

   Reasons _____

   _____

   _____

6. Jeff and Jack are in two different public speaking sections. They work together on a speech describing how the Pyramids were built. Each gives essentially the same speech in his speech class.

   Jeff and Jack (have) (have not) plagiarized.

   Reasons _____

   _____

   _____

7. For her speech on the importance of fastening seat belts, Leigh reads a pamphlet on the 5 most popular excuses for not fastening seat belts. Since the excuses are written in a clever, catchy style, Leigh uses the words from the pamphlet when talking about excuses in her speech.

   Leigh (has) (has not) plagiarized.

   Reasons _____

   _____

   _____

■ Other Legal/Ethical Issues

Although the following legal violations occur much less frequently than plagiarism in the public speaking classroom, students should be aware that speakers can and do break laws designed to protect innocent parties. The first category of illegal speech is **defamation**. **Defamation** occurs when a speaker makes claims against a person's character that cannot be supported with evidence. Defamation is more than the occasional humorous joke about a politician. Defamation claims have the power to damage the person's reputation, and they are not founded on facts.

The second legal issue is based on potential harm for audience members rather than harming an individual who is the target of the speaker's ill will. This second category falls under the label of **clear and present danger**. The classic example is calling "fire" in a crowded theatre. Anything the speaker says that has real potential to endanger the lives of audience members may fit into this category. One can make an argument that speeches advocating sniffing glue to get high or building a "beer bong" so that one can consume a very large amount of alcohol in a short time fit into the endangerment category.

The third subcategory under legal/ethical considerations comes into play when a speaker advocates that audience members **break the law**. Speeches on creating fake i.d.'s and how to avoid getting a speeding ticket (implying that listeners should break the speed laws) are examples. A speaker may believe a law is unjust, speak against that law, and also encourage audience members to help change the law; but directly or indirectly recommending that laws be broken is not ethically appropriate for public speakers.

Rhetorical Sensitivity

A speaker who is **rhetorically sensitive** is concerned about the feelings of the audience members. Such a speaker will be honest and direct but will avoid saying things that embarrass, wound, or exclude audience members. Many speakers do not deliberately set out to make members of the audience uncomfortable or isolated, but do so because they make the faulty assumption that everyone in the audience has the same attitudes and beliefs as the speaker does. When students speak on topics of religion, they often assume that everyone in the audience is a Christian or at least has a Christian background. Some students, especially international students, have been raised with a very different spiritual orientation. The speaker may speak from a Christian viewpoint, but needs to be sensitive to deeply held beliefs and practices of some audience members who do not have a Christian belief-system or background. Political issues are also a realm where the speaker may make false assumptions about audience attitudes.

Rhetorical sensitivity is especially important on gender and sexual topics. Speakers need to be sure they do not send messages that can be interpreted as sexual harassment. Bashing either gender is not appropriate. When speakers address sexual orientation issues, they must do so in a rhetorically sensitive manner. Sometimes speakers talk about sexual matters in what they think is a joking manner. Class members may laugh, but many feel uncomfortable about a speaker bringing a "stag-party" atmosphere into the classroom.

Speakers must always be sensitive about making judgements about beliefs, attitudes, values, and groups of people. Statements of judgement must have impeccable support—not just vague hints or unsupported or unwarranted insults.

ACTIVITY **3.6**
Legal, Ethical, and Audience Considerations for Speeches

Choose the best answer or answers for each situation given below. Be able to explain the reasons for your choice orally to the class.

1. Mike brings his boa constrictor into class in a closed box, puts the box on the table as he begins his speech. He speaks for about thirty seconds, then quickly brings out the snake and thrusts it toward the audience members in the front row. Mike laughs and says, "Now that I have your attention, I'll speak about how to balance your checkbook."

    Was Mike's speech beginning a violation of

    A. Legal/Ethical Responsibilities

    B. Rhetorical Sensitivity

    C. None of the above

    Reasons: _____

    _____

2. Elaine uses as her Thesis for a speech, "I will convince my audience that Jesus Christ was real and not merely a myth."

    Is Elaine's speech a violation of

    A. Legal/Ethical Responsibilities

    B. Rhetorical Sensitivity

    C. None of the above

    Reasons: _____

    _____

3. Kyle gives a speech in which his Audience Outcome Goal calls for a behavioral change to safe sex. During his conclusion, he hands a condom to each audience member.

    Is Kyle's distribution of condoms to all audience members a violation of

    A. Legal/Ethical Responsibilities

    B. Rhetorical Sensitivity

    C. None of the above

    Reasons: _____

    _____

4. Liz tries to persuade her audience to purchase a device that warns them when law enforcement officers are using radar to monitor speed so that her fellow students can drive above the speed limit without getting speeding tickets.

   Is Liz's message to her audience a violation of

   A. Legal/Ethical Responsibilities

   B. Rhetorical Sensitivity

   C. None of the above

   Reasons: _____

   _____

5. Harold asks his fellow students to sign a petition requesting that a law be introduced and passed to lower the drinking age to 18.

   Is Harold's action a violation of

   A. Legal/Ethical Responsibilities

   B. Rhetorical Sensitivity

   C. None of the above

   Reasons: _____

   _____

6. Jennifer claims that intercollegiate football should be abolished because football players do not have the necessary intelligence to be students, are law breakers, and are dangerous because of their violent personalities.

   Is Jennifer's message a violation of

   A. Legal/Ethical Responsibilities

   B. Rhetorical Sensitivity

   C. None of the above

   Reasons: _____

   _____

■ Preparing for Your First Speech

At this point, you have been introduced to the major components of speech building: Decision Factors, Global Decisions, and Local Decisions. However, you have not yet had the opportunity to practice applying the extensive procedures and advice to the construction of an actual speech. If you remember the introductory analogy about comparing a prepared speech to building a house, you recognize that this is the point at which the text stops focusing on that grand ideal speech and drops down to provide practice on different types of Support Materials.

The first support material category is **Narration**, and a Narration Speech will be your first assigned speech. As you prepare this first oral assignment, you should begin by considering the Decision Factors that apply to the speech situation; then make the Global Decision of Topic Selection, Audience Outcome Goal Statement, and Thesis Statement. Because this is a short assignment, primarily using just one type of Support Material, you may not need or be able to divide the speech into Main Points. In effect, the claim that you label as the Thesis may be the one Main Point of the speech.

You will have the opportunity to practice identifying and developing Main Points in future speeches that have longer time requirements. At this time, your instructor may ask you to review this chapter. But for this first assignment, the purposes are to learn in depth about one kind of Support Material while practicing Global and Local Decision making at the most basic level.

■ Key Concepts

Listed below are some key concepts from this chapter. Test yourself by seeing if you can explain and give examples of each.

- audience need to know
- oral speech thesis
- secondary speech goal
- mutual inclusiveness
- audience outcome goal statement
- planning thesis
- primary speech goal
- main points
- cognitive changes
- subordinate points
- affective changes
- support materials
- behavioral changes
- plagiarism
- claims
- rhetorical sensitivity
- thesis statement

Chapter Study Guide

You should be able to:

- List and identify four *Global Decisions.*

- Give guidelines for choosing a speech topic.

- Define the following terms and be able to identify examples of each: *Primary Speech Goal, Secondary Speech Goal, Audience Outcome Goal Statement, Audience Cognitive Changes; Audience Affective Changes,* and *Audience Behavioral Changes.*

- Give guidelines for and be able to write an *Audience Outcome Goal Statement.*

- Define the following terms and be able to identify examples of each: *Claims, Thesis, Planning Thesis, Oral Speech Thesis, Main Points, mutually inclusive nature of Thesis and Main Points.*

- Give guidelines for and be able to write a *Thesis Statement.*

- List and identify three *Local Decisions Categories.*

- Define and be able to identify examples of the following: *Supporting Claims, Subordinate Points,* and *Support Materials.*

- Illustrate graphically or through a metaphor the relationship of *Topic, Audience Outcome Goals, Thesis, Main Points, Subordinate Points,* and *Support Materials.*

- Explain the term *"Plagiarism"* as it applies to classroom speeches and be able to identify whether or not a speaker has plagiarized.

- Explain the terms *"defamation," "clear and present danger," "advocating audience break the law,"* and *"rhetorical sensitivity"* as they apply to classroom speeches and be able to tell whether or not a speaker has violated these legal/ethical standards.

ASSIGNMENT
Report of Outside Speech 1: Global Decisions

This report will be based on a live speech (not taped, television, or radio) that you will have experienced no more than a week prior to the date the assignment is due. Possible live speeches include classroom lectures (not in this class), sermons or homilies, guest speakers at organizations or in public forums, work-related training lectures or motivational speeches. There are, of course, other possibilities. You may not use a student speech from a class. The report should be typed and be *no more than two pages long*.

Your report will include the following:

1. Information about the **Speaker**, name, credentials.

2. Information about the **Setting**: location, time of day, size of room, special physical problems in the room (such as temperature, visibility of speaker).

3. Information about the **Audience**. number of people present, reasons why they have chosen to attend, level of enthusiasm for speaker and speech, degree of similarity of audience members (same age? gender? level of education? job or career experiences?).

4. Information about the **Global Decisions**:

    Topic: stated topic, narrowed topic, fit of topic to assignment and context factors, fit of topic based on speaker's expertise, fit of topic to audience based on audience needs, fit of topic to physical setting.

    Speech Goals: Primary Audience Outcome Goals stated by speaker or assumed from context, Primary Outcome you experienced; Secondary Outcomes either stated or experienced.

    Thesis: Thesis either stated or extracted from speech by you, presence or absence of narrowed topic and how topic would be developed.

    Main Points: Main Points either stated or extracted from speech by you, wording strategies used to label Main Points, mutually inclusive relationship of Main Points to Thesis Statement.

5. Write a paragraph analyzing how the **Global Decisions** you have identified influenced your understanding, interest, and retention of the speech.

UNIT **2**

Support Material

CHAPTER 4
Narration

Chapter Objectives
After reading the chapter you should be able to:
• Describe the advantages of using Narration.
• Explain the characteristics of the narrative categories of Case Study, History, and Story.
• Explain the three narrative components of Plot, Characters, and Setting.
• Give examples of how Narration may be used in speeches.
• Present a Narrative Speech that includes appropriate explanatory material and uses effective presentational techniques.

■ Introduction to Narration

When most people hear the term "**Narration**," they tend to think first of **Stories** or anecdotes, but there are other support materials that fit under the general heading of narrative. Two additional subcategories of Narration that are especially useful in speeches are **Case Studies** and **Histories**. Although stories, case studies, and histories differ from each other in several important ways, they all include the **Essential Narrative Elements** of (1) movement through time and (2) change. Telling what happened in the order it happened is an old and natural pattern of human communication.

■ Advantages of Narration

Narration is an excellent choice for speechmakers because this type of support material is especially good for (a) creating easy-to-follow speech structure, (b) promoting memory of structure and content, (c) enhancing interest, and (d) providing variety within the speech. Both the speaker and listeners have the time pattern to guide them. This simplifies speakers' organizational decisions and gives them a sequential framework as a memory tool when presenting the scenes and details of the narrative. The audience moves along the path of time with minimal effort and can actively participate in and remember the narrative.

Narratives appeal to audiences because the tales often remind listeners of their own experiences, and the time pattern, at least, is predictable. At the same time, narratives keep audience attention because the outcome of the narrative is uncertain. "Will it end the way I expect it to, or will there be a surprise twist?"

An additional benefit of Narration is that the speaker can use it to change the mood or rhythm of a speech. Narratives take longer to present than support materials such as statistics or example. Listening to a longer, more leisurely support, serves as a rest for the audience. In addition, audience members often think of a narrative as a reward within a speech. When the speaker tells a story or develops a case history, the audience expects that they can sit back and enjoy this part of the speech since they will not have to work hard at understanding or learning the content. Since narratives often focus on human characters, they allow the speaker to humanize and personalize an abstract or dispassionate subject. When a speaker wants to create an emotional moment, he or she will probably choose narrative.

Types of Narration

The subject of the Narration and the events relayed are somewhat different for the three subtypes of narrative. Both **case studies** and **histories** focus on real events; **stories** may be either non-fictional or fictional.

Case Studies

Case Studies are the products of deliberate study of an individual. The individual does not have to be a person but might be an organization, a group, or a natural phenomenon. The changes that happen to the individual are observed or analyzed to learn about, or explain, the larger set the individual represents. When a speaker uses a case study of one patient's progression through the stages of a disease to explain the symptoms and treatment of that disease to the audience, the goal is to allow the listeners to learn about the disease rather than just to discover what happened to the one patient.

Histories

The possible subjects for histories are similar to those given for case studies: the life history of individual people, organizations, or a natural phenomenon. In the case of history, the real experiences are chosen not because the individual is representative, but because the experiences form a complete narrative of the chosen subject. Consequently, the history may include data from many sources and viewpoints. While case studies primarily represent reporting of factual information in a time-change pattern, histories are free to include opinions and judgements.

Stories

Stories and anecdotes share some features with each of the other categories of narrative. Like the case study, stories in speeches promote understanding and learning by standing for something else. However, instead of serving as a typical example of all similar experiences as case studies do, stories serve as support for abstract ideas or concepts. Stories do not have the same limited one-to-one relationship of representation that exists for case studies. The same story may fit to illustrate more than one "moral."

Stories, like histories, lack the elements of scientific selectivity and control characteristic of case studies. Neither is limited to just the facts. Stories are enhanced by detail and comment.

ACTIVITY **4.1**
Types of Narration

Compare the following examples of Narratives to the characteristics of *Case Studies*, *Histories*, and *Stories*. Decide which type of Narrative each description best fits.

1. Kathleen has as her claim: "you never know how much you can do until you are challenged." She tells what happened, how she felt, and how she reacted when the flood waters threatened her house during the summer of 1998.

    Type of Narration: _____

2. Juan wants to illustrate the importance of preparedness for natural disasters. He tells about the Great Flood of 1998 from the first rains until cleanup was over. He uses a variety of sources for his narrative: newspaper accounts, interviews with eyewitnesses, statements from experts.

    Type of Narration: _____

3. Louise is arguing that her university should adopt the Quarter System rather than continue on the Semester System. To support her claim, she tells of the experiences State U. had when they changed from the Semester to Quarter System.

    Type of Narration: _____

4. Brad is informing the audience about the career of Occupational Therapist. He takes them through a typical day of an Occupational Therapist.

    Type of Narration: _____

5. Marie tells a Hopi folk tale to make the point that all people in a community are important.

    Type of Narration: _____

6. Karl describes and explains the breakup of European countries into small, ethnic states before World War I to warn his audience that they should be concerned about the recent changes and conflicts in Europe today.

    Type of Narration: _____

■ Components of Narration

Typically, narratives will be composed of a **Plot**, **Characters**, and a **Setting**. Other types of support material, especially description, may include characters and setting, but Narration is unique because it has a plot. In narrative, something always happens or changes.

Plot

The organizational structure of a narrative is time related. Since time and change are inevitably bound together, the organizational structure of narrative follows that of a sequential series of changes as they occur over time. At some point in the story, history, or case study, the teller informs the listeners what happened first, second, and so on.

A catalogue of events in order is not automatically interesting. Listeners are drawn into a narrative because of the nature of the changes. "The plot thickens" because of *complications*. The building up of small events or changes and their relations to each other arouses curiosity. What do they mean? What will be the outcome? Is the narrative building toward a surprise? OR are the events building toward an inevitable result from which there is no escape?

The final event or change in the narrative plot is the *resolution*. Now the outcome or solution is shared with the audience. With the resolution comes a reaction—surprise, relief, laughter, sorrow. The speaker may use that reaction to reinforce the application of the narrative to the claim being supported.

Characters

Part of the appeal and emotional impact of narrative is the focus on characters, which allows the listeners to find a point of concrete personal identification. Not all characters are people. Especially in a history or case study, the central character might be an organization, institution, a place, or even an object. Nevertheless, non-human characters are often treated as if they are human or at least have human attributes. Storytellers may talk of change in inanimate subjects with the human terms of birth, growth, death, learning, thinking, and feeling.

Setting

Not only are narratives located in time; they occur within specific physical locations. The "when," "where," and "what happened before" aspects of the narrative give audiences the necessary background to locate "what happens now." The speaker enriches the narrative experience by including details and descriptions of the setting.

■ Where and How to Use Narration in Speeches

Narratives can be used in almost any part of a speech. The only recommendation for locating a story, history, or case study in a speech is that the narrative fulfill the function of appropriately supporting the specific idea or concept the speaker has decided to promote in that part of the speech. Some speakers find an amusing story, and although it has no connection with the subject or themes of the speech, decide to tell it during the speech just because it is a good story. Telling an unrelated story is a risk since it may interrupt the continuity and cohesion of the speech. Some audience members may be distracted as they try to discover the meaning of the story and its place in the speech. If the speaker openly admits the irrelevancy, he may lose less credibility as a skillful speech builder, but he has still diminished his commitment to the chosen topic by throwing in a "red herring."

Narration in Introductions and Conclusions

Speakers commonly use stories or histories in the introduction of a speech for the following reasons: (1) to promote interest, (2) to illustrate and personify the significance of the topic, (3) to create a sympathy for the topic, or (4) to provide background information to enhance understanding of the topic. In the conclusion of the speech, stories serve these functions: (1) to summarize the content of the speech, (2) to provide an emotional focus, (3) to serve as an effective memory tool to reinforce the Claims of the speech, and (4) to leave the audience with a sense of closure.

You may be familiar with the technique of "bookend" stories. Here the same story is used in both the introduction and conclusion, providing a frame for the speech, just as a pair of matching bookends encloses a row of books. There are two common methods of using "bookend" stories. The speaker may tell the whole story in the introduction and then only refer to it again as part of a final plea in the conclusion of the speech. Or an alternative strategy is to tell part of the story in the introduction and "the rest of the story" in the conclusion.

Another popular device used in stories for introductions and conclusions is a "visualization" story. Here the speaker may ask the audience to close their eyes and let the voice of the speaker take them on an imaginary trip or through an experience. This technique allows the audience to become more deeply involved in the story as they add their own details and concentrate on the story itself since some sensory distractions have been removed.

Narration in the Body of the Speech

Within the body of a speech, telling a story is an excellent technique to regain diminishing interest. As you look at the types of Support Materials you plan to use, try to balance some necessary, but perhaps less interesting, strategies with more compelling support from stories or case studies. By playing factual or statistically-rich sections off against the longer, less-demanding technique of narrative, stories provide an opportunity for audiences to rest and relax. Stories, especially those with high emotional content, are very persuasive

and can be used to supplement logical arguments when the Audience Outcome Goal is to promote a change of belief or a change in behavior.

Narrative Structure for a Full-Length Speech

In addition to using narrative within the speech, the speech builder has the option of using Narration to create the overall structure of a fully-developed speech. There are at least two ways to go about this. First, the entire speech may consist of one history, case study, or story that the speaker has subdivided into parts for the audience. The second approach is to use a different history, case study, or story to illustrates the idea or concept of each Main Point.

The first method is especially appropriate if the subject is the life of a person or the history of something. Speakers often divide biographical or tribute speeches into time-related segments of the person's life such as (1) early influences, (2) early adulthood achievements or choices, and (3) mature successes or changes. The history of almost anything—an invention, a movement, a war, a corporation, a relationship—can be divided up into a beginning, middle, and end (or high point).

A less obvious structure that grows out of narrative occurs when a story contains a series of lessons. The speaker may present the story in the introduction and identify the ideas that will become the Main Points. Since the Main Points are both derived from and given initial support from the story, the audience has a very tidy memory device for retaining the structure of the speech both while it is being developed and when they leave the experience.

The second approach of multiple narratives works best for a relatively short speech that covers material familiar enough to the audience that the speaker does not need other types of Support Material to explain or define new ideas or processes. A series of stories or case studies exemplifying the Main

■ Key Concepts

Listed below are some key concepts from this chapter. Test yourself by seeing if you can explain and give examples of each.

- case studies

- histories

- stories

- essential narrative elements

- plot

- complications

- resolution

- characters

- setting

- bookend stories

Chapter Study Guide
You should be able to:
• Identify the two essential elements of *Narration*.
• List three advantages of narrative as *Support Material*.
• List and differentiate the three categories of *Narration* and give an example of each.
• Identify and briefly explain the following: *Plot, Complications, Resolution, Characters,* and *Setting*.
• Give guidelines for how and where to use narrative in a speech.
• Explain two methods of using narrative to structure an entire speech.
• List four types of explanatory information that may accompany a narrative.
• Prepare and orally present a narrative.

ASSIGNMENT
Narration

Length: Between 2 and 5 minutes

Task: Tell a story, case study, or history that illustrates an idea or concept. At some point in the presentation, you need to identify for the audience the Claim or Thesis is being supported. Also include other explanatory information such as necessary background information.

Note Restrictions: You may use one 4 × 6 notecard if you wish. You are not required to use any notes, but if you choose to do so, please turn the notecard in when you finish speaking.

Preparation: You will fill out and turn in the "Speech Planning Sheet." In addition, you should practice and time the narrative as you plan to present it in class.

Speech Planning Sheet

1. What is your primary Audience Outcome Goal for this assignment?

   _____

   _____

2. What is the Claim/Thesis the narrative supports?

   _____

   _____

3. What part of a complete speech would this narrative be used in?

   _____

   _____

4. What was the length of the presentation in your final practice? _____ minutes.

Instructor's Evaluation of Narration

Speaker identified Claim/Thesis and
explained relationship of narrative and
Claim/Thesis

_____

Narrative was an appropriate choice for
supporting Claim/Thesis

_____

Auxiliary explanations contributed to overall
effectiveness

_____

Progress of events was logical and easy to
follow

_____

Character development enhanced narrative

_____

Language choices contributed to effectiveness

_____

Narrative maintained audience interest

_____

Speaker maintained a natural, conversational
delivery style

_____

Speaker used voice and body to increase
understanding and interest

_____

Speaker refrained from distracting voice and
body behaviors

_____

Speaker maintained eye contact

_____

Peer Evaluation of Narration

Name of Speaker _____ Your Name _____

Speech Topic _____

Listening For Content

1. What did you think was the Claim/Thesis of the speech? _____

   _____

2. What did you think was the Audience Outcome Goal? _____

   _____

3. Which type of narrative did the speaker use? story _____ , case study _____ , history _____

   Give one reason for your choice. _____

   _____

   _____

Listening For Evaluation

1. What part of the narrative was most effective and why? _____

   _____

2. What delivery aspect (how the speaker looked and sounded) was most effective and why?

   _____

   _____

3. Name one thing that would have improved the speech. _____

   _____

CHAPTER 5
Definition

Chapter Objectives
After reading the chapter you should be able to:
• Explain how Definition may be used to increase understanding, and appreciation for language, and to persuade audiences.
• Distinguish between Descriptive and Prescriptive Definitions in order to locate appropriate definitions.
• Identify the parts of a definition that represent Classification and Differentiation and use this understanding to create definitions.
• Identify and be able to use the Definitional Strategies of Verbal Examples, Sensory Examples, and Secondary Definitions.
• Recognize what terms need to be defined.
• Prepare and present Definitions in Speeches.

Use of Definition

It is very common for speakers to define unfamiliar terms near the beginning of their speeches in order to provide critical background and understanding for listeners. Definition for understanding is necessary to clarify the speaker's meaning of familiar terms that may be ambiguous due to multiple meanings or application of the term in a situation or manner new to the audience. **Definition** is the act of sharing the meaning of specific terms with an audience. It is used most often to promote the audience outcome of understanding. Definitions can also be used to (a) persuade, (b) gain appreciation for language while developing vocabulary, or (c) entertain.

When speakers are trying to convince an audience to accept a belief, they may choose to define a term in such a way that it supports the speaker's viewpoint. For example, a pro-choice advocate on the abortion issue might chose a clinical definition of abortion that states that "abortion is a medical procedure that terminates pregnancy before the fetus is capable of survival as an individual." On the other hand, a pro-life advocate's definition might be "abortion is the act of killing unborn children." An entire speech can be based on the premise that if the audience accepts the speaker's definition, they will accept the conclusion of the speech.

Speakers who enjoy words and language may wish to share their understanding and appreciation of a special word or term with an audience.

This approach is sometimes developed into a complete speech that includes (1) the etymology (history and origin of the word), (2) examples of use, and (3) stories that epitomize the meaning. Exploration of unique terms usually results in a speech of high interest for the audience because of the novelty of the information. Some speakers use a technique that on the surface appears to be definition to amuse or entertain the audience. Comedians throw out absurd one-line definitions that hit just close enough to home to get a laugh. "Diplomacy is the art of saying 'Nice doggie,' while looking for a big rock."

Origin of Definitions

Definitions fall into two categories related to the origin of the definition: (1) descriptive definitions and (2) prescriptive definitions. **Descriptive Definitions** reflect the established and conventional usage of a word. The meaning of the word has come about by informal consensus of those who use the term. The person who records the definition is just describing an already agreed-upon meaning. **Prescriptive Definitions** are commonly created for brand-new terms. For example, when a new technology arises, the language needed to talk about the inventions or developments is chosen by those who invent or work with the technology. In addition, new observations, such as scientific discoveries of previously unknown phenomenon, and the exploration of new theories require specialized terms that must be carefully and precisely defined.

Think of all the terms related to computers that did not exist a few years ago. Before computer technology became common, the word "mouse," using the descriptive definition from common usage, meant "a small rodent." Early computer equipment developers also prescribed that "mouse" would mean the external plastic instrument for moving a cursor or arrow on the computer monitor.

When a speaker consults a dictionary in preparation for explaining the meaning of a term in a speech, it is helpful to know whether the definition of a term is based on common usage or whether the definition was explicitly created for a term. This will help the speaker decide what type of dictionary to use. Most general usage dictionaries such as *Webster's, American Heritage,* or *Random House* contain primarily descriptive definitions. Some dictionaries, such as *Oxford English Dictionary*, show not only contemporary usage of terms, but chronologically present the changing meaning of terms as they were commonly used throughout history. However, when a speaker is using a term that has been coined and defined for special use in such areas as medicine, law, and technology, then the speaker should go to a specialized dictionary to find the prescriptive definition. A list of special topic dictionaries is found in Appendix A, "Library Research Methods."

How to Define Terms

Classification and Differentiation

If you ask someone to give you a definition or scan through a dictionary looking at definitions, you will find that most word explanations, whether they are based on description or prescription, follow the same format. This common approach to explaining terms is called **Classification and Differentiation**. Try defining the term "knife." Most students begin with "a knife is a tool..." or "a knife is an instrument..." This part of the definition is the **Classification**. Out of all possible categories, the definition limits "knives" to the class of "tools" or "instruments." The rest of the definition tells how knives are different from other tools or instruments. You may have defined "knife" by its *use*: "a knife is an instrument used for cutting things" or by its *characteristics*: "a knife is an instrument with a sharp blade." You may have included both use and physical description since the **Differentiation** needs to be complete enough so there is no possibility that a knife will be confused with a sword, a pair of scissors, or a razor. The definition of "knife" from *The American Heritage Dictionary* illustrates sufficient differentiation: "A cutting instrument consisting of a sharp blade with a handle."

Another technique for establishing differentiation between terms is *comparison/contrast*. It is difficult to find a concrete description of some characteristics. For example how can one describe the characteristics of the color red? A speaker can use words like "hot" or "bright" but those words do not provide a mental picture of "red," nor do they tell the difference between "red" and "yellow." The best way to establish the difference of red from other colors is to use some type of comparison, either by naming a synonym or describing similarities to something the receiver already knows. "Red is the same color as scarlet." "Red is a warm color similar to orange but with less of a yellow tone." Notice that the comparison to orange also includes contrast: how red is different from orange.

When you decide to use a definition in a speech, a good strategy is to first go to a dictionary to check your accuracy of understanding. Then recast the definition in your own words using classification and differentiation. If you wish to use the words of the dictionary, then at least identify the class and how differentiation has occurred. This will help you make the definition more your own, and you will avoid the common problem of definitions being presented in classroom speeches by the speaker going on "automatic pilot" and reading the words without showing understanding or meaning.

ACTIVITY **5.1**
Practice Definitions

Practice defining the following common terms using *Classification and Differentiation*. Remember to (1) identify the overall class and (2) identify how the term differs from others in the same class. Three ways to differentiate terms are by (1) use and function, (2) descriptive characteristics, and (3) comparison/contrast.

Notice which strategy or strategies you use to create differentiation.

1. *egg beater* _____

    definition strategy _____

2. *mother* _____

    definition strategy _____

3. *walk* _____

    definition strategy _____

4. *happiness* _____

    definition strategy _____

▨ Additional Definitional Strategies

As you defined the terms on the previous page, you may have discovered some problems. Defining "egg beater" by use often leads to simply repeating what you are trying to define: "An egg beater is an instrument used to beat eggs." The abstract nature of "happiness" makes it difficult to settle on just one description for the feeling or to find one synonym that captures exactly the level of feeling. Some people believe that to define "mother" as a "biological female parent" is too limited and sterile. "Walk" has more than one meaning depending on whether you are talking about an action or a place.

Two excellent techniques to further clarify and extend the audience's understanding and appreciation of terms beyond classification/differentiation definitions are (1) exemplification and (2) secondary definitions of categories, parts, or terms that make up the primary term.

Verbal Examples

Examples work as verbal shorthand that create a vivid, easily remembered image of the term. It is helpful to follow a dictionary-type definition with one or more *exemplars and non-exemplars.* An "exemplar" is an example, but not just any example; it is a model, archetypical example. A speaker might use an extended example of an individual who personifies the essence of what "mother" means to that person.

A "non-exemplar" is also an example, but this time the speaker is giving an example of what the term is not. "An egg beater is not a fork, even though a fork may be used to beat eggs." Non-exemplars are needed when the speaker knows that many people have misconceptions about the term. "An agnostic is not a person who denies there is a god, but a person who does not *know* whether there is a god or not."

Sensory Examples

For some terms, the best example is one the audience can see, hear, touch, smell, or taste. To really understand the differentiating characteristics of "impressionist" painting, an audience needs to see examples of paintings that show the brush strokes, the colors, and the overall impression. Using words alone to define "curry" just is not enough. Audience members must smell or taste the spices of curry powder to have a complete definition. Samples of taped music extend audience perception and understanding of heavy metal music. The speaker has an advantage over the writer since an oral communicator can supplement verbal examples with sensory examples.

Secondary Definitions

Some terms are best defined by defining typical subcategories or parts that make up the whole term. A speaker could attempt to expand an audience's understanding of a familiar term such as "happiness" by defining several different types of happiness: "exhilaration," "contentment," "joy." An acronym such as AIDS is often defined by subdefinitions of each of the terms that make up the whole term: "acquired," "immune," "deficiency," "syndrome." Words with multiple meanings (such as "walk") or homonyms, words that sound alike but are spelled differently and have different meanings, (such as "raise" and "raze") may require more than one definition to reduce confusion and establish which meaning the speaker is using.

Use the following activity to practice using definition techniques.

ACTIVITY **5.2**
Classification/Differentiation of Dictionary Definitions

Instructions: For each of the following definitions, underline the class once and the differentiation twice. Tell whether differentiation is by (1) use, (2) characteristics, or (3) comparison/contrast. Include as many of these techniques as apply.

1. *grotesque*: a style of decorative art characterized by fanciful or fantastic human and animal forms often interwoven with foliage or similar figures that may distort the natural into absurdity, ugliness, or caricature.

   Techniques _____

2. *resistor*: a device that has electrical resistance and that is used in an electric circuit for protection, operation, or current control.

   Techniques _____

3. *cerumen*: the yellow waxy secretion from the glands of the external ear—called earwax.

   Techniques _____

4. *mildew*: a superficial usually whitish growth produced on organic matter or living plants by fungi.

   Techniques _____

5. *serendipity*: the faculty of finding valuable or agreeable things not sought for.

   Techniques _____

Pick out two of these terms and tell how you would use example(s) to expand on the definitions. If you choose verbal examples, give at least one exemplar and one non-exemplar.

_____

_____

_____

_____

_____

■ What Should Be Defined?

There is no point in spending speaking time talking about a word or term unless you have some new information or insight about the term to share with the audience. A definition should not be just filler. Many of the terms used as examples previously are not good candidates for definition in a speech. A speaker probably will not extend the listeners' understanding and appreciation of familiar terms such as "knife," "walk," or "red." On the other hand, students occasionally take the challenge of an in-depth word study that results in both speaker and audience learning more about an ordinary term we use every day.

More often though, speakers define terms which are new or misunderstood by audiences. The editors a recent edition of *The American Heritage Dictionary* have added "more than 10,000 new general vocabulary words" and "more than 5,000 new scientific and technical terms" since the first edition published in 1969. One of the goals of this dictionary is to reflect the changing language of America, and those 15,000 plus new words illustrate why definition is such an important element in communication. To the right you will find examples of contemporary or unfamiliar terms arranged by categories. These examples illustrate the type of terms speakers need to define within major speeches and also may help you select a term to define for the group definition assignment.

Medical	Political/Social/ Economic
lyme disease	political correctness
eating-right pyramid	racial quotas
laser surgery	gender-neutral language
arthroscopic surgery	conservative
	liberal
	muni bonds
	chapter 11 bankruptcy
	balkanization
	hurried child syndrome

Technical	Arts and entertainment
fuel-injected	cubism
ergonomics	oxymoron
"smart" bombs	infomercials
anti-lock disc brakes	

Vocabulary-building	Slang
halcyon	home boy
plethora	dis
	phat
	my bad
	spamming

■ Key Concepts

Listed below are some key concepts from this chapter. Test yourself by seeing if you can explain and give examples of each.

- descriptive definitions

- prescriptive definitions

- classification

- differentiation

- verbal examples

- exemplars

- non-exemplars

- sensory examples

- secondary definitions

Chapter Study Guide
You should be able to:
• Give examples of how *Definition* can be used for each of the following Audience Outcome Goals: (1) audience will increase understanding, (2) audience will be persuaded, (3) audience will be entertained, and (4) audience will increase appreciation.
• Define and identify examples that illustrate *Descriptive Definition* and *Prescriptive Definition*, and discuss the importance for a speaker knowing whether a term is descriptive or prescriptive.
• Define and identify examples that illustrate the part of definition that is called *Classification* as well as the part of definition that is called *Differentiation*.
• List and briefly explain three methods of *Differentiation*.
• Define and identify Examples that illustrate *Verbal Examples, Exemplars, Non-exemplars, Sensory Examples,* and *Secondary Definitions*.
• Give guidelines for what terms should be defined in speeches.
• Prepare and orally present *Definitions* in speeches.

ASSIGNMENT
Definition (Group Speech)

Length: Between 3 and 5 minutes

Task: Four speakers will present oral definition(s) of a word or term following the structure of introduction, development of definition, and conclusion. Within the development phase, the speakers may use several techniques to define the same term. Group members must first choose a term to define. Together they plan an introduction, development, and conclusion for a speech that defines their term. Each speaker orally presents some part of the speech. One student may present the introduction, a second gives part of the development, a third the rest of the development, and the fourth presents the conclusion.

Note Restrictions: Speakers may use one 4 × 6 notecard if they wish. Speakers are not required to use any notes, however, at the conclusion of the speech, each speaker is required to hand in either the notecard, a brief outline, or map of the part of the speech he or she presented. During the oral presentation, speakers must cite any outside materials used as sources of definitions.

Preparation: Each group member will fill out and turn in the "Speech Planning Sheet." In addition, individuals should practice and time their part of the speech as they plan to present it in class.

Speech Planning Sheet

1. What is the word or term being defined? _____

2. What is the Audience Outcome Goal? _____

   _____

   _____

3. What is the Claim (Thesis) being developed in the speech? _____

   _____

   _____

4. What Definitional Techniques are used? _____

   _____

   _____

   _____

5. What is the significance of this term for the audience? (Why should they learn about this term?) _____

   _____

   _____

   _____

6. What outside sources did you use to research the term? _____

   _____

   _____

   _____

   _____

7. How long was your part of the speech in the final practice? _____ minutes.

Instructor's Evaluation of Definition

Speaker established an appropriate audience "need to know"   _____

Speaker clearly shared Claim (Thesis)   _____

Speaker orally shared plan of development   _____

Speakers selected effective definitional strategies   _____

Speakers cited outside sources   _____

Speakers maintained audience interest   _____

Speakers followed the overall speech plan of introduction, development, conclusion   _____

Speech moved toward realization of Audience Outcome Goal (understanding, appreciation, entertainment, persuasion)   _____

Individual Speaker Delivery

Speaker maintained a natural, conversational delivery style
Speaker 1   Speaker 2   Speaker 3   Speaker 4

Speaker used voice and body to increase understanding and interest
Speaker 1   Speaker 2   Speaker 3   Speaker 4

Speaker refrained from distracting voice and body behaviors
Speaker 1   Speaker 2   Speaker 3   Speaker 4

Speaker maintained eye contact
Speaker 1   Speaker 2   Speaker 3   Speaker 4

Speaker projected confidence
Speaker 1   Speaker 2   Speaker 3   Speaker 4

Instructor's Evaluation of Definition

Speaker established an appropriate audience "need to know" _____

Speaker clearly shared Claim (Thesis) _____

Speaker orally shared plan of development _____

Speakers selected effective definitional strategies _____

Speakers cited outside sources _____

Speakers maintained audience interest _____

Speakers followed the overall speech plan of introduction, development, conclusion _____

Speech moved toward realization of Audience Outcome Goal (understanding, appreciation, entertainment, persuasion) _____

Individual Speaker Delivery

Speaker maintained a natural, conversational delivery style
Speaker 1   Speaker 2   Speaker 3   Speaker 4

Speaker used voice and body to increase understanding and interest
Speaker 1   Speaker 2   Speaker 3   Speaker 4

Speaker refrained from distracting voice and body behaviors
Speaker 1   Speaker 2   Speaker 3   Speaker 4

Speaker maintained eye contact
Speaker 1   Speaker 2   Speaker 3   Speaker 4

Speaker projected confidence
Speaker 1   Speaker 2   Speaker 3   Speaker 4

Sample Speech Planning Sheet

1. What is the word or term being defined?   *Autumn*

2. What is the Audience Outcome Goal?

   Understanding, appreciation, entertainment

3. What is the Thesis being developed in the speech?

   The definition of the term "autumn" depends on the background of the person who is

   using the term

4. What definitional techniques are used?

   Classification/differentiation.

   Exemplification: verbal and sensory:

   Secondary definitions (defining sub-classes)

5. What is the significance of this term for the audience? (Why should they learn about this term?)

   It is a term most people know but they do not understand its origin or how it is used by

   different people; my speech will help the audience have more understanding of the word,

   especially next Wednesday, the first day of autumn.

6. What outside sources did you use to research the term?

   The Oxford English Dictionary.

   Encyclopedia of Word and Phrase Origins.

7. How long was your part of the speech in the final practice?   *2 minutes*

■ Sample Note Card for Entire Speech

Introduction:

Opener: *Story of radio announcer mentioning next Wed. is first day of autumn and thinking about how I always say "fall."*

Significance for Audience: *Although very well-known term, there is more audience can learn about it and appreciate, timely since next Wed. is first day of autumn.*

Thesis (and Preview): *I will explain the meaning of "autumn" from three different perspectives; first, a technical definition; second, calendar definitions related to location; third, a personal definition. (def. of sub-classes.)*

Development:

I.   *Astronomical Definition—"from the descending equinox to the winter solstice." (on map show position of sun and date for equinox and winter solstice) (different) (classification)*

II. *Calendar Definition—"the third season of the year, or that (comparison/contrast) between summer and winter" Sept. 21 to Dec. 21*

    A.   *North America—Sept., Oct., Nov.*

    B.   *Great Britain—Aug., Sept., Oct. (verbal examples,)*

    C.   *France—end of Aug. to first two-weeks of Nov.*

    D.   *Southern hemisphere—same as spring in northern hemisphere*

III. *Personal Definition—not a set of dates, but a set of characteristics*

    A.   *Weather—crisp, not cold, sun or rain, not snow, windy*

    B.   *Clothes—sweaters, sweaters, sweaters, not shorts or scarves*

    C.   *Activities—football, not baseball, walking, riding, school (verbal examples)*

    D.   *Food—cider, apples, chili, doughnuts*

    F.   *Feelings—pleasantly melancholy, invigorated.*

SUMMARY AND CONCLUSION:

Next Wed. remember it is the first day of autumn because of the location of the sun, but in Great Britain and France, autumn started last month and won't start in the southern hemisphere for six months. Here in North America it will start for me when the weather, clothes, food and feeling tell me it is "autumn."

CHAPTER **6**
Description

Chapter Objectives
After reading the chapter you should be able to:
• Explain the role of Observation in description.
• Identify Physical Properties by using sight, hearing, smell, taste, and touch of a place, structure, object, or living organism.
• Explain how to organize a Description using four different patterns.
• Distinguish between Concrete, Specific Language and Abstract, General Language.

■ Chapter Overview

The term Description comes from the Latin verb "describere," meaning, "to delineate." One of the definitions given in the *American Heritage Dictionary, 2nd College Edition* for "description" is "the act of drawing or tracing a figure." Because speakers and writers use "describe" to include everything from a story to an emotion ("Let me describe what happened," "It's hard to describe how I felt"), it is useful to go back to an earlier emphasis given to the term "description" in order to separate out (draw a line around) just what is meant when we talk of Description as a Support Material in discourse.

For the description activity in this class, limit your description to the *physical properties* of what you are describing. You will create a mental picture for the audience of the aspects that can be perceived only by *human senses*. Whatever you choose to describe must be limited to what you can see, feel, touch, taste, hear, or smell. Four common categories for descriptions are (1) places, (2) structures, (3) objects, and (4) living organisms.

■ Observation

In order to prepare for this activity, you need to do what the artist does first when "drawing or tracing a figure." You need to use your senses to study the object of your description. In some cases you may choose to describe a place, person, or thing which is currently inaccessible to you. In that case, you will have to search your memory for the sensory details.

Begin making a list of descriptive details of the subject you plan to describe for the class. The details you discover by a deliberate sensory exploration should be categorized and recorded under appropriate sense categories. Use the chart provided later in the chapter to record your impressions. Don't let the chart limit you; at this point restrict yourself to only those physical properties you can experience through one of the senses.

Visual

There are many physical aspects that depend on the sense of sight. Ask yourself the following questions about what you see.

1. What parts make up the whole? Include how those parts fit together.

2. What materials or substances are present? What is/are the thing or things you are describing made of?

3. What color(s) are present? Include shades, hues, locations.

4. What shape(s) are present? Note both external and internal aspects and regular and irregular shapes.

5. What level of reflectivity is present? Dull? Shiny? Elements of both?

6. What size is/are the thing(s) you are describing?

7. Is this a two-dimensional or three-dimensional object?

8. Does the item being described look different from different locations?

9. Do the physical aspects of the thing you are describing resemble the physical aspects of something else you can use as a comparison?

10. What other visual aspects do you notice?

Aural

Sometimes the sounds associated with an object or place seem such an integral part that we automatically include them in a description. I wouldn't describe my alarm clock without mentioning that repetitive, high-pitched, electronic chime. Places and structures may be inundated with a plethora of sounds. Even a structure like an empty church, which initially seems silent, may be a reservoir of murmurs, echoing street sounds, creaks, and pops. A place such as a crowded city street or a favorite restaurant is so full of sounds that the observer has a difficult time sorting them out.

It may be more difficult both to record on paper sounds for your description and to find words that represent those sounds. Keep in mind—your description is *not primarily how the sound makes you feel* but *what you hear.* Below are some questions that may help you identify and express the physical properties of what you hear.

1. What rhythmic sound patterns are present? This includes both individual sounds and combined and overlapping sounds.

2. What pitches do you hear? Low? High? Medium?

3. What are the volumes? Loud? Soft? Medium?

4. What is the duration of the sounds? How long do they last? How long is the silence?

5. What is the quality of the tones? Round? Full? Thin? Raspy? Mixed?

6. Is the nature of the sound related to its origin and is there an adjective that expresses that relationship? Bell-like? Buzzing? Humming? Purring? Electronic? Clanging? Siren-like?

7. What can you compare the sound(s) to?

8. What other aural aspects do you notice?

Smell

Scents and odors can be very evocative physical properties. When you smell a certain perfume, burning leaves, or home-baked cookies, those smells evoke a flood of memories and emotions. Check on the physical characteristics of smell when preparing your description.

1. What is the essential nature of the smell? As with sound, the dominant nature may be related to the origin of the smell. Sweet? Metallic? Pungent? Acrid? Spicy? Smokey?

2. What is the intensity of the smell? Strong? Subtle? Elusive? Overpowering?

3. What is the duration of the smell?

4. What can you compare the smell to?

5. What other aspects of smell do you notice?

Taste

The physical properties related to taste may be less important when describing many topics such as sight, sound, and smell. However, if the speaker is describing a food or drink, taste becomes a central focus of the physical description. We are told that the taste sense basically reports if something is sweet, sour, bitter, or salty. All other aspects of what we think of as taste are perceived through smell or touch. Part of the pleasure of some foods comes from the combination of taste, smell, and texture.

1. Is the taste sweet, sour, bitter, or salty?

2. What is the overall nature of the "taste"? Here also origin may help to label the primary property. Fruity? Creamy? Dry? Tangy?

3. What can you compare the taste to?

4. What other aspects of taste do you notice?

Touch

This final category contains a variety of sensory properties that seem quite different from each other but have the common bond of the sense of touch. The discoveries that we make about texture, weight, density, temperature, and pressure all are related to touch,

1. What is the texture? Smooth? Rough? Gritty? Slick?

2. What is the weight or density? Heavy? Light? Heavy for its size? Light for its size?

3. What is the temperature? Hot? Cold? Warm? Cool? Frigid?

4. What level and type of pressure is exerted? Gentle? Painful? Continuous? Intermittent? Crushing?

5. What can you compare to any of these touch properties?

6. What other touch sensations do you notice?

Physical Properties of _____

Visual	Aural	Smell	Taste	Touch
Parts	Rhythms	Nature/origin	Sweet, Sour, Bitter, Salty	Texture
Composition	Pitch	Intensity	Overall Nature	Weight/Density
Color	Volume	Duration	Comparison	Temperature
Shape	Duration	Comparison	Other	Pressure
Luster	Tone Quality	Other		Comparisons
Size	Origin			Other
Comparison	Comparison			
Other	Other			

Creating a Description

If you have devoted time and effort to observation, you now have a comprehensive set of data about the physical properties of whatever you plan to describe. At this point, the speaker needs to do some sorting and prioritizing. The goal is to create a vivid mental picture for the audience. You may be tempted to create the verbal equivalent of "sensorama" and bombard the audience with sensory recreations. You will probably be more successful in moving toward the goal if you call on a variety of the senses, but since this is a speech, not a "happening," you need to select the data that will best produce a cohesive, meaningful image.

Content Decisions

As always when planning, the speaker starts with deciding on the Audience Outcome Goals and Central Claim. Within a speech, description is often designed to produce some kind of emotional reaction—nostalgia, sympathy, delight, horror. That emotional response may be tied to a more general goal of persuasion or appreciation. Description also can play a valuable role in understanding and memory. An expository description may be necessary to understand a technical object, a historical structure, or the geological forces that have changed a place. Memory is enhanced when the emotional and the rational are both involved. We remember places, objects, buildings, and people that we have experienced clearly and that we have also experienced in an emotional way.

The speaker selects and rejects data from observations based on what information best develops and supports the two Global Decisions of Audience Outcome Goals and the Thesis.

Organizational Decisions

There are several patterns of organization that complement description: (1) spatial categories, (2) parts, whole, and their relationships, (3) sensory categories, and (4) time order.

Spatial Categories

Structures, places, and objects lend themselves well to a spatial or geographical organization of the information. For example, the speaker can organize the physical properties into those observed at the top, middle, and bottom. Other spatial categories are: (a) inside and outside, (b) left to right, and (c) center to periphery.

Parts, Whole, and Their Relationships

Focusing on one of the component parts at a time and then moving on to the next part is similar to a spatial organization, but here the relationship of parts with each other and with the whole object adds an additional component. Another variation that emphasizes the parts and whole is a description that moves from a general description to description of specific details.

Sensory Categories

Sensory categories include such subdivisions as: (a) how it looks, (b) how it sounds, (c) how it smells, (d) how it feels, and (e) how it tastes. The speaker certainly does not need to include all five senses. To keep the overall image from becoming too fragmented, the speaker should reintegrate the physical properties during the conclusion so the listeners are left with a composite picture.

Time Order

Using a time sequence based on a gradual discovery of the properties is another overall organizational frame a speaker can select. For this assignment, speakers need to be careful not to step over the line into narration when using this approach for description. The focus is not on "what happens" but on the features of what is being described. The speaker is not required to choose any of these patterns to structure the description. However, it is recommended that the speaker have a plan for the composition of the mental picture rather than producing a random collage.

Language for Description

The most important guideline for selecting the words you will use for description is to choose *concrete, specific language* over *abstract, general language*. By their very nature, general, abstract terms do not create pictures in our heads. An activity that illustrates the picture-making power of concrete words and specific details is building what General Semanticists call a **ladder of abstraction**. The ladder is a continuum of descriptions of the same thing from the most abstract to the most concrete.

Most Abstract

A thing

A living organism

An animal

A carnivore

A cat

A male adult Siamese Cat

My 17-year-old Siamese cat, Koko, who has blue points and a loud meow

Most Concrete

Key Concepts

• physical properties

• spatial categories

• parts, whole, and their relationships

• sensory categories

• concrete, specific language

• time order

• abstract, general language

Chapter Study Guide
You should be able to:
• List 4 common categories for *Description* topics.
• Give 4 guidelines for preparing a description.
• List and be able to recognize examples of the 4 common patterns of organizing description.
• Prepare and present description in speeches.

ASSIGNMENT
Description

Length: Under 3 minutes

Task: Speaker will present an impromptu description of a place, structure, object, or organism emphasizing the physical properties of what is being described. The goal is to create a vivid mental picture for the audience. As an introduction, the speaker presents a brief claim or thesis statement, which should identify what is being described. In the introduction the speaker should also establish the relevance of the description for the audience. The speaker must choose a pattern of organization that guides the audience easily through the description. The speaker should conclude with a summarizing statement which reminds the audience of what was described and the organizing principle the speaker used to present the description.

Note Restrictions: You may choose to use notes or not.

Preparation: You will fill out and turn in the "Speech Planning Sheet."

Speech Planning Sheet

1. What is the Audience Outcome Goal? _____

    _____

2. What is the Claim or Thesis being developed in the speech?

    _____

    _____

3. Is the subject for description a structure _____ place _____ object _____ or organism _____ ?

4. What pattern of organization has been chosen for the description?

    _____

5. What is the significance of the topic of description for the audience?

    _____

    _____

Sample Speech Planning Sheet

1. What is the Audience Outcome Goal?

    Appreciate the beauty and grandeur of the prairie.

2. What is the Claim or Thesis being developed in the Speech?

    The western prairie has a unique aesthetic appeal that can be appreciated from

    a wide panoramic view: from a mid-distance view and close-up.

3. Is the subject for description a structure _____ place _X_ object _____ or organism _____ ?

4. What pattern of organization has been chosen for the description?

    Spatial, periphery to center, also sensory categories.

5. What is the significance of the topic of description for the audience?

    Audience members live near the prairie, but may not know the appealing features

    of the prairie so that they can enjoy this unique land area.

■ Sample Notecard

Introduction:

Opener: *Explain about plans for Prairie National Park as a tourist attraction.*

Significance for Audience Members: *Members live near a unique land area, but may not be familiar with it, nor enjoy and appreciate it.*

Claim or Thesis: *The western prairie has a unique aesthetic appeal that can be appreciated from a side panoramic view, a mid-range view, and a close-up view.*

Body (Development):

I. *Wide Panoramic View—see horizon, hills and valleys, sunsets, patchwork quilt of fields and pastures, seas of grass; hear distant sounds of traffic.*

II. *Mid-range View—see cottonwood trees, rock outcroppings, deer grazing, birds overhead; hear bobwhite calling, the wind.*

III. *Close-up View—see wild flowers, variety of grasses, rabbits, rocks with fossils in them, tracks and droppings of animals, butterflies, moths, other insects; feel the warm sun and soft breeze; hear birds and insects; smell the scents of flowers, cool musty air in damp places, the clean dry air on hilltops.*

Summary And Conclusion:

Whether one experiences the prairie from a great distance, a mid-range distance or close up, there are many things to see, hear, and smell that make the prairie a place of variety, beauty and tranquility.

Instructor's Evaluation of Description

Speaker established an appropriate audience "need to know"   _____

Speaker clearly shared Claim (Thesis)   _____

Speaker included properties related to several senses   _____

Speaker primarily used concrete, specific language, including comparisons   _____

Speaker for most part avoided extensive narration, reports of feeling, reactions, and judgments   _____

Speaker used an appropriate organizational structure   _____

Speaker maintained audience interest   _____

Speaker followed the speech plan of introduction, development, conclusion   _____

Speech moved toward realization of Audience Outcome Goal (understanding, appreciation, entertainment, persuasion)   _____

Speaker left audience with a clear vivid mental picture   _____

Speaker maintained a natural, conversational delivery style   _____

Speaker used voice and body to increase understanding and interest   _____

Speaker refrained from distracting voice and body behaviors   _____

Speaker maintained eye contact   _____

Speaker projected confidence   _____

Instructor's Evaluation of Description

Speaker established an appropriate audience "need to know" _____

Speaker clearly shared Claim (Thesis) _____

Speaker included properties related to several senses _____

Speaker primarily used concrete, specific language, including comparisons _____

Speaker for most part avoided extensive narration, reports of feeling, reactions, and judgments _____

Speaker used an appropriate organizational structure _____

Speaker maintained audience interest _____

Speaker followed the speech plan of introduction, development, conclusion _____

Speech moved toward realization of Audience Outcome Goal (understanding, appreciation, entertainment, persuasion) _____

Speaker left audience with a clear vivid mental picture _____

Speaker maintained a natural, conversational delivery style _____

Speaker used voice and body to increase understanding and interest _____

Speaker refrained from distracting voice and body behaviors _____

Speaker maintained eye contact _____

Speaker projected confidence _____

UNIT 3

Using Support Materials to Build Complete Speeches

■   Using Support Materials to Build Complete Speeches

CHAPTER **7**
Building a Complete Speech

Chapter Objectives
After reading the chapter you should be able to:
• Apply what you have learned about Decision Factors, Global Decisions, and Local Decisions to the preparation of a complex speech.
• Explain the relationship of Lower Level Supporting Claims and Support Materials to developing the Body of the speech.
• Discuss appropriate choices for selecting and placing Support Materials.
• Explain the three parts of an Introduction and what may be included in each.
• Explain what should be included in the Conclusion.
• Explain the role and construction of Internal Transitions.
• Provide an overview of all component parts of a complete speech.
• List the steps a speaker follows to move from a speech plan to the speech that is presented to the audience.

■ Overview of the Chapter

Up to this point in the course, the speaking assignments have been short speeches utilizing fairly simple structure or organization. The remaining speech assignments require that speakers thoroughly understand the Global Decisions, and faithfully apply the guidelines for (1) choosing Topics, (2) writing Audience Outcome Goals, (3) writing a Thesis, and (4) constructing the Main Points, in order to construct complex speeches that are both audience-centered and have an easy-to-follow pattern of organization. This chapter will (1) review the roles of *Decisions Factors*, *Global Decisions*, and *Local Decisions*, (2) expand on *Local Decisions* that have not been previously covered (Lower Level Supporting Claims, Introductions, Conclusions, and Internal Transitions), (3) present a process for combining the parts of the speech into a final speech plan; and finally, (4) present the process speakers use to turn the plan into the extemporaneous speech that is presented to an audience. Before you study the new information in this chapter, you may benefit by going back to Chapters 2 and 3, and reviewing the topics of Decision Factors, Global Decision, and Local Decisions.

Roles of Decision Factors, Global Decisions, and Local Decisions

As you remember from earlier in the course, the speaker begins to prepare a speech by identifying and analyzing *Decision Factors* that influence the preparation and presentation of a speech. In the early stages of speech preparation, the speaker tests the *Global Decisions* of Topic Selection, Audience Outcome Goals, Thesis, and Main Points against context/assignment factors and audience background factors to make sure that the final product, the speech itself, will be consistent with the assignment and fit the specific audience. Once a speaker has solidified the Global Decisions, then the foundation of the speech plan has been created and the speaker is ready to continue researching the speech in preparation for making *Local Decisions.*

When you prepare your speeches, always be sure to *write* out your Thesis, Audience Outcome Goals, and Main Points so you will have written guides in front of you as you continue to plan the speech. In the next section, we will discuss the Local Decisions that are made after the speaker has chosen Main Points. These are speaker decisions related to developing and supporting each Main Point of the body of the speech.

Creating the Body of the Speech

Many speakers have a desire to write down what they plan to say in the speech body. At this point in the process of speech preparation, the speech builder should not write a word-for-word manuscript of the speech. In fact, we highly recommend that the speaker never write down the exact words of the speech since using an extemporaneous manner of speaking is more effective than a speech that is read or recited from memory. Instead, while the speech is being created, the speaker should prepare a *planning outline* or *planning map* that will serve as a record of how each Main Point will be developed. The planning

outline is not the same outline or set of notes the speaker will write on a notecard to use while delivering the speech. More information about the extemporaneous mode and the notecard are covered later in the chapter.

The *planning outline* or *planning map* is a graphic representation of the speech claims and support for the claims the speaker plans to use. The claims are organized in descending order from the most general to the most specific claims. It should be noted that the actual order of presenting the information while delivering the speech might be different from that of the planning outline/map.

Lower Level Supporting Claims

As you constructed and presented your first few speeches, it is possible that you decided on Main Points and then expanded on those concepts in a general way without specifically planning or structuring how you would support those claims. From this point on in the course, you will be expected to follow an explicit plan of subdividing Main Points into *Lower Level Supporting Claims* and/or *Support Materials*. These Lower Level Supporting Claims must represent natural divisions of the Main Points they support. Keep in mind that all supporting claims must represent ideas or concepts, not concrete information.

The organizational pattern of claims that creates the skeleton of the speech may be compared to a pyramid, a web, or a family tree. You begin with the most general claim, the **Thesis**. The Thesis is neatly subdivided into your **Main Points**. Each Main Point may be subdivided into two or more **Supporting Claims** and each Supporting Claim may be divided again into **second level Supporting Claims**. For most classroom speeches, your speech plan of claims will not go below the second level of Supporting Claims. When a speaker creates an outline to represent the organizational plan of the speech, the Main Points are shown as Roman numerals (I, II) and the first-level

Supporting Claims are shown by capital letters (A, B). The author may also need to use Supporting Claims at the next lower level. The proper symbol to use for second level Supporting Claims is an Arabic numeral (1, 2). As you create the frame for the body of your speech, you will arrive at a point where your next level is not a claim but is instead concrete information. This then falls into one of the Support Material categories such as a story, factual evidence, a definition, or description. At that point, the speech builder should stop dividing and focus on the selection and placement of Support Materials.

Support Materials

As speakers have thought about, talked about, and researched the overall speech, they will have started to collect at least a mental file of possible *Support Materials* such as: narratives, descriptions, explanations, definitions, examples, lists (of stages, criteria, symptoms), quotations, and specific facts. After an outline or map of the claims for the speech body representing at least two levels has been created, the speaker should tentatively go through the map or outline and assign at least one piece of support material to the final supporting claim in each sequence of claims. This is the most efficient time for the speaker to write down the sources of any outside information that need to be credited when the speech is presented orally.

When making the support material assignments, the speaker will check to see that the most appropriate support has been chosen. Does the explanation or evidence really support the claim? Is the emotional tone appropriate for the location of the support within the speech? Is a piece of high interest support needed at some point in the speech to regain audience interest? Has the speaker created variety by using as many different kinds of support as possible?

Good places to introduce original support materials created by the speaker, such as comparisons, hypothetical examples, and visual aids, are: (1) obvious holes you discover in your speech or (2) sections where the speech is losing momentum. Once the speech begins to take shape, the speaker may want to consider two other support factors (1) overall support themes or structures such as narrative or overarching metaphors and (2) memory strategies.

Both Global and Local Decisions up to this point have been primarily related to the Body of the Speech. Only after the plan for the Body is well developed is the speaker in a position to prepare the Introduction and Conclusion. Premature decisions about how to start or conclude the speech may no longer fit after the speechmaker has constructed, revised, reordered, and refocused the main part of the speech. In addition, the speech composer may uncover the perfect support materials for the introduction and conclusion when sifting through support for the body.

■ Introductions

Introductions consist of three main parts: (1) the opener, (2) introduction transition, (3) statement of Thesis and preview of Main Points. These three elements combine to promote the **Purposes of Introductions**: (1) arouse curiosity about the topic and provide motivations for listening to the speech, (2) provide background information about the topic and speaker, (3) provide the audience with the plan of the speech, and (4) give the audience an opportunity to become familiar with the speaker.

Opener

The primary goal of the Opener is to draw the audience into the speech. Several approaches work well to stimulate audience interest and commitment to staying with the speech. The sooner audience members become active participants in the speech the greater the chances are of capturing and keeping the audience. Consequently the speaker will choose to begin with high interest, concrete material that intrigues the audience by arousing such reactions as curiosity, personal concern, emotional response, or simply a friendly association with the speaker and/or topic. Audiences will leave (mentally) as soon as the speech begins if the speaker's first words are abstract generalizations that seem to have no personal connection for the listener. Do not begin with a generalized summary statement or an announcement of the topic. Metaphorically take the hands of the audience and lead them into the topic with specific statements.

Because you are already familiar with support materials, you have a menu of powerful techniques to use as you begin to speak to the audience. **Narrative** is almost always a good choice, especially if the speaker personalizes the story so there is some direct association for the listeners that they can connect to their own experiences or situations. Some speakers create the opportunity for direct audience participation in an opener story by taking the audience on a narrative mind trip. Narratives by their very nature include the element of suspense. Because audiences want to know "how it all comes out," they will effortlessly stay with a story.

Speakers create a different kind of audience participation opener by composing a series of **questions** that they direct toward the audience for overt answers or comments. A similar technique is to ask the audience to *do* something. Listeners will begin to mentally ask "why?" and "where is this going?" and become curious and involved.

Any relevant **statement that surprises** the audience will also serve as an interest arouser. This is especially true when the statement has a direct connection to or association with the audience or the situation. Sometimes speakers establish the "need to know" or motivation for listening by sharing new and compelling statistics about the frequency of a problem or phenomenon—the number of people struck by lightning last year, the number of overweight Americans, the probability that audience members will have to work two jobs to support themselves.

Inexperienced speechbuilders may make the mistake of producing over-dramatic, exaggerated openers that do more harm than good. Speakers do not have to "grab" the attention of the audience because they already have just by walking to the front of the room. They just have to sustain it and let it grow. If the opener is misleading or overpowering, the audience will never get beyond the opener to the speech itself. The speaker who brings in a boa constrictor and thrusts it toward the audience and then says "Now that I have your attention, I'll explain to you how to balance your checkbook," has, at the worst, alienated the audience and, at the best, distracted them.

A well-crafted opener logically leads to the disclosure of the subject of the speech. The announcement of the speech topic (but probably not the Thesis) often occurs at the very end of the opener and provides the logical, natural bridge to the next part of the introduction, the transitional section.

Introduction Transition

Many students plan to include transitional material in the introduction and intuitively feel it fits best immediately after the opener. However, some speakers just go from the opener immediately to the Thesis and preview. That is too abrupt, and audiences are not given the information they need before the speaker moves on to the heart of the speech. This section of the introduction also serves, as the label "transition" suggests, to provide the connection between the opener and the plan of the speech presented in the Thesis/Preview. Some business that speakers take care of in **Introduction Transitions** are: (1) the general background about the topic such as history, explanation, definitions, (2) the relevance of the topic for the audience, and (3) the background of the speaker.

The need to include preparatory background information often becomes clear to students when they are building complete speeches. They discover there are unfamiliar terms that the audience needs to know, that the audience needs a working acquaintanceship with the major characteristics of a phenomenon or disease, or that the audience will appreciate the subject more if they have some knowledge of the history of the phenomenon, disease, or process. The tendency is to make the definition, characteristic identification, or history into a 30-second Main Point. These brief presentations of information really aren't major divisions of the body that result from the Thesis, but are background material that should go in the transition section of the introduction.

It makes good sense to provide the audience with a strong motivation for listening to the speech near the beginning rather than at the end of the speech. You have been practicing sharing the significance of your speech content with the audience as you have presented short speeches using support materials. You may have discovered that you have to stretch to find a personal practical application for every audience member for every topic. An alternative is to establish significance by showing how the information has a major impact (widespread, costly, dangerous) on the society in general of which audience members are a part. The following activity, "Relevancy for Audience," will give you an opportunity to practice discovering audience significance.

ACTIVITY **7.1**
Relevancy for Audience

For each of the following potential speech topics, tell what the speaker could say in the introduction to answer the question, "Why should this audience listen to a speech on this topic?"

You are to demonstrate significance for the audience in *two ways*: (a) how the information affects audience members personally and (b) how the information impacts society in general. This second significance is usually established by consulting an outside source. Your instructor will either ask you to go to the library to look up statistical information or expert opinion about the frequency, serious nature, or widespread impact of the phenomenon *or* your instructor will give you permission to *invent for this assignment only* examples of information from outside sources to demonstrate significance.

1. virus that causes common cold

    a. _____

    _____

    b. _____

    _____

2. the status of the Social Security system in the U.S.

    a. _____

    _____

    b. _____

    _____

3. the past, present, and future of rap music

    a. _____

    _____

    b. _____

    _____

Speakers can enhance their personal credibility during the introduction and at the same time create a friendly atmosphere for the speech by including some personal information about themselves. Some speakers establish common ground between themselves and the audience members by referring to similar background experiences, especially those that relate to the topic. Speakers may even tell how they became interested in the topic, emphasizing the common elements that should inevitably lead to similar audience interest in the subject.

The speaker may want to send the double message of "I am just like you," but "I am also different because I am now an expert on this topic." It is a good idea to always share with the audience the source of your expertise. Speakers can establish, without bragging, that the audience should have confidence in what is said by emphasizing the process of how they gained the knowledge—through study, work experience, observation, experimentation, or practice.

Transitional portions of introductions take many different forms depending on the topic, speaker, and audience. There is no set formula or specific checklist of required elements; a speaker should say whatever is needed to prepare the audience.

Plan of Speech

The last section of the introduction is short and straightforward. The speaker needs, in an obvious manner, to announce the Thesis and preview the Main Points. Word cues warn the audience that the plan of the speech is coming. Many speakers use such phrases as: "today I will talk about …" or "I want to share with you this morning my views on…" Whatever words you choose, plan them ahead of time and make your announcement so blatant that no one can fail to reproduce your Thesis. Help the audience identify the Main Points by using number words: "I will analyze this topic by examining *three* probable causes; *first…*"

■ Conclusion

The Conclusion of the speech is almost the mirror image of the introduction. After speakers have finished developing the final supporting claim, they begin wrapping up the speech by reiterating the Thesis and summarizing the Main Points. Usually it is not necessary to repeat lower level claims. The audience will remember the basic structure and important ideas of the speech longer if the speaker repeats the same key phrases in the summary that were used in the preview and body of the speech for the claims. It is also a good idea to "wave a red flag" for the audience that lets them know the review and summary are next. "Let me summarize what we have covered today." "In conclusion…"

Once the business of storing the frame of the speech away in audience memory is complete, then the speaker needs to finish out the experience for the audience with an appropriate Closer. The closer is both a signal ("That's all, Folks!") and the speaker's last chance to get the message to the audience. Plan a final statement that accomplishes both of these functions but does not introduce new, irrelevant ideas.

Like the Opener, this last section of the speech will probably be constructed from specific concrete materials. A story or "the rest of the story" will let the audience comfortably know the speech is over while reminding them one more time what you would like them to take away from the speech. Some speakers make a final appeal for the audience to use the experience in some way. Others try to find some unique way to encapsulate the total wisdom of the speech in a final statement. Some speakers fall back on "Thank you" as a way to stop the speech. If there has been something extraordinary about the experience that causes you to want to say a special word of appreciation to the audience, then do thank them, but don't throw in a meaningless "Thanks" just so you can go back to your seat.

Internal Transitions

Repetition is an important technique to promote retention of the speaker's message. Ideally, an audience will leave your speech and be able to reproduce the essential elements of that speech because they will have heard the skeletal elements of the speech at least three times: in the preview, in the final summary, and in the internal transitions. Internal transitions also provide audiences with updates of where they are in the speech.

Internal Transitions are found at each major division in the body of the speech. When speakers conclude the development of the *first* Main Point, they give a one-sentence transition. The sentence will include the key **summary** phrase of what was presented in the first Main Point and a key **preview** phrase of what will be presented in the second Main Point. "Now that we have explored *the first cause of an astronomical, military spending, national debt run-away inflation*, we'll look on to a *second cause of the debt, pork-barrel allocations*." This same process of short summary and short preview should be repeated between each pair of Main Points.

Putting the Speech Together

The parts of the speech in the order you will present them are summarized below. In this example the speaker uses three Main Points. You may choose to use between two and five Main Points.

Introduction

- Opener

- Introduction Transition

- Thesis and Preview

Body

- Development of Main Point 1

  Internal Transition

- Development of Main Point 2

  Internal Transition

- Development of Main Point 3

Conclusion

- Restatement of Thesis and Summary

- Closer

This representation of speech parts shows the major components that the speaker will present, but it is still not the speech the speaker will give. How do you get from this generic list to your own individual speech? Speechbuilders can insert the written records of the Global and Local Decisions they have already made into the appropriate locations on the list. Brief notes or outlines of each of the three parts of the Introduction will be written first. The Thesis and Preview may be written out word for word. Transfer the development of each Main Point from the planning outline or map and create internal transitions between each pair of Main Points. Then the speaker's notes or outline for the Conclusion finishes off the tentative speech that is now starting to take form.

Preparing to Speak Extemporaneously

Going from the Speech Plan to the Speech You Present

Once a written plan of all the elements of a speech has been completed, the speaker is ready for the last four steps of speech preparation: (1) oral drafting to discover the words of the speech; (2) oral practice to discover what needs to be revised; (3) making a notecard and (4) final polishing of the speech with attention to delivery elements.

Oral Drafting

When preparing a speech that will be delivered **extemporaneously**, a speaker does not write out the speech word-for-word as one does for a speech given in the **manuscript** or **memorized modes**. Instead the speaker discovers the text of the speech by talking through the speech several times. This process is called **oral drafting**. Here is the simple process you should follow to create the words of your speech. (1) Find a place where you can be alone. (2) Silently, read over your entire speech plan. (3) Relying on your written plan, talk through each part of the speech out loud. At this point, don't worry about mistakes or struggles to find words. Exact time is not important in this first run-through. You will probably start, stop, and repeat. When you have talked through the entire speech once, you have a rough oral draft of your speech.

Oral Practice for Revision

From this first try at turning the speech plan into a speech, you may have discovered some problems with the speech. If so, you should revise your plan before you try to give the speech again. This is a good time to consider major changes such as reorganizing the speech or adding or deleting large segments of the speech. Be sure to alter your written speech plan. Now using your revised written plan as a guide, try to give the speech orally from start to finish again, incorporating the changes you have made. This second oral draft will probably be smoother, and you will find you are moving closer to your finished speech. During this second rehearsal, you should time the speech.

After the second session, once again check for improvements that need to be made and once again make those changes on your speech plan. Keep revising and creating oral drafts until you are satisfied that you are close to the speech you want to give.

Making the Notecard

It is only after the speech is pretty well set that you will make your notecard. The notecard is for you; so write on the notecard only what will be useful to you when giving the speech. Do not write out complete sentences, nor worry about proper outline form. Usually phrases and key words are enough to jog your memory when you need help. It makes good sense to write down specific information you are apt to forget such as statistics, direct quotations, or specific names. The notecards from this text are designed to help you write down what you need to know in the order you will need the information. Some speakers use highlighters to help them find information on the notecard when they are speaking. For example, the speaker may highlight all main points in yellow; all source citations in blue; all statistics in green. When you suddenly forget the name of a source, you will just have to look for words that are highlighted in blue at the appropriate point in the speech.

Final Polishing

After the notecard is prepared, the speaker should then practice the speech as many times as needed in order to speak fluently and feel comfortable and confident. The number of practices required varies from person to person.

There is a danger that when a speaker goes over and over a speech, the words will become so set that the speaker in effect has created a memorized speech. When this happens, a speaker's delivery may lose the natural and spontaneous sound it should have to appeal to an audience. To prevent a speech from becoming too scripted, speakers should consciously use slightly different words each time they go over the speech. This practice giving a "new" speech in each practice means that since you have practiced a variety of ways to express each idea, you will also have a menu of possible words available if you have a memory lapse while speaking.

In addition to polishing the content of the speech in these later practices, the speaker should also be aware of delivery behaviors. During these sessions, the speaker should stand, gesture naturally in response to the content of what is being said, be sure words are pronounced correctly, and check to be sure voice volume is appropriate.

Once you have a good final practice, leave the speech alone. Your speech preparation is finished. You may want to go over your notecard just before class to remind yourself of the order of content, but do not repeatedly practice the speech in your head while waiting to share your speech with the audience.

ACTIVITY **7.2**
From Plan to Speech

Below are illustrations of the steps a speaker goes through when creating the oral draft of the speech and revising through oral practice and polishing the speech. Create a label for each step. Be able to orally explain what the speaker would do in each of the steps of the process.

1 _____

2 _____

3 _____

4 _____

5 _____

6 _____

7 _____

8 _____

9 _____

Key Concepts

- opener
- introduction transition
- relevancy for audience
- plan of speech
- internal transitions
- extemporaneous mode

Chapter Study Guide
You should be able to:
• Explain the general process of speech construction referring to the following *Global Decisions:* topic selection, audience outcome goals, thesis, and main points.
• Explain the function and pattern of a *planning outline* or *planning map*.
• Complete the explanation of the general process of speech construction referring to the following *Local Decisions*: 2nd and 3rd level supporting claims (subordinate points), and support materials.
• List and briefly explain or define the 3 parts of an *Introduction*.
• List 4 functions of *Introductions*.
• Give 2 guidelines for content of Introduction *Opener* and 3 examples of strong content choices a speaker could use for an *Opener*.
• List 3 types of information speakers may share in *Introduction Transitions*.
• List and give examples of 2 types of *Relevancy* for the Audience that speakers use.
• Identify what speakers should include when sharing *Plan of Speech* with the audience.
• Identify what speakers should include in the *Conclusion* of the Speech.
• Identify the two elements of *Internal Transitions* and where in the speech *Internal Transitions* should be presented.
• List the elements and subelements of a speech in the order the speaker will present them.
• Give guidelines for writing a notecard.
• Give guidelines for practicing a speech.
• Prepare and present a complete speech.

CHAPTER **8**
Comparison

Chapter Objectives
After reading the chapter you should be able to:
• Explain the two types of focus or viewpoints of comparison.
• Distinguish between *Same Class Comparison* and *Different Class Comparison*.
• Describe the characteristics of three types of comparison speeches.
• Explain the process for selecting a topic for a comparison speech.
• Create audience outcome goals and thesis statements consistent with each of the three types of comparison speeches.
• Explain the divided and alternating patterns for organization comparison speeches.
• Discuss how to select appropriate comparison items.
• Identify the unique functions of comparative language.
• Give examples of ongoing metaphors.

◼ Chapter Overview

Comparison can be an unusually effective speaking tool for helping an audience to understand a new concept and for persuading an audience to accept a speaker's proposal. This chapter is divided into three sections: (1) defining and clarifying the term Comparison as it is used in this text; (2) explaining three types of Comparison Speeches; and (3) creating Comparison Speeches.

◼ Defining and Clarifying Comparison

Levels of Comparison

Comparison is the process of putting two things side by side either mentally or physically and observing the features shared in common by both objects. A person may choose to compare any number of things, objects, ideas, concepts or processes. It is important to note that the **focus or viewpoint** used when comparing may be based either on (1) our overall impression of the two items as a whole, or (2) the parts or features of the two. For example, when we compare a rubber ball and an orange, our general impression of the two as whole objects is that they are similar since they are both spheres. However, if we shift our focus to the specific features of these two round objects, we identify such differences as the ball bounces, the orange does not, and the ball is filled with air, the inside of the orange is made up of pulp and juice. In this case although the two appear to be similar as a whole, a closer look at the parts shows us significant differences.

Same Class and Different Class Comparisons

When we carefully analyze two objects, people, ideas, or processes, both to compare them as a whole and to compare specific characteristics of each, we find each pair fall into one of three patterns. Some comparisons reveal that the pair has similar features for both the whole and the parts such as a chicken and a duck. Others disclose that the whole of the two is similar, but the specific features are different (a live duck and a stuffed toy duck), and finally the opposite, the whole or external features are different, but the two have some significant parts or features in common (a chicken and a coward). Comparisons are divided into (1) **Same Class Comparisons**, those in which the pair seem alike at first glance, and (2) **Different Class Comparisons**, those that initially are seen as very different from each other when observed as a whole.

When a communicator uses a *Same Class Comparison*, sometimes called a "literal comparison," there is an immediate recognition of similarity, at least on the surface, because the two fit into the same general class of objects or ideas. Regardless of whether the parts or specific features are alike (the chicken and duck) or different (the live duck and stuffed toy duck), if on the whole the two items seems to be alike, then the pair is classified as **Same Class Comparison**. An example of a Same Class Comparison where both the whole and parts are similar is when a speaker compares the roles of individuals in a business to the roles of individuals in a family. In both cases *roles people play in groups* is the class. Same Class Comparisons are often used to teach about something that is remote or unfamiliar by looking at something local and well-known from the same class such as comparing the federal budget to your household budget.

A second type of Same Class Comparison is that for which the whole or external features are alike, but closer examination shows the parts or specific features have important differences. Both Jupiter and Mars fit into the general class of planets, but their features of size, color, chemical makeup, topography, temperature, and activity differ dramatically.

Strangely enough, some excellent comparisons are made between pairs that on the surface appear radically different, but when studied from the specific level, it is discovered that they have at least one important part or characteristic in common (chicken and coward). Such comparisons are called **Different Class Comparisons**. An example of a Different Class Comparison is the comparison of human arteries and water pipes in a house to explain circulatory disease. They are from different classes since clearly one is living tissue and the other is a manufactured metal object However, they are both a hollow cylinder and unwanted substances can adhere to the inside wall of each and cause the inside circumference to decrease resulting in decreased flow of liquid.

Different Class Comparisons include "figurative comparisons" such as those found in poetry and cliches or folk-sayings. "Those two children are as alike as two peas in a pod." "I'm as mad as a wet hen." Part of the impact of such comparisons is the awareness of the contrast of radically different first images of the two followed by recognition that one or more of the relevant characteristics of the pair are actually strikingly similar.

■ Types of Comparison Speeches

When an observer concludes the two things are alike because of the similarities, especially the parts, a comparison of the two can be used as a very effective explanatory technique in speeches. Sometimes when studying the two phenomena, it is discovered that although the two resemble each other in many important ways, there are also significant differences, again usually the features discovered from analysis. In this case, the comparison may be used by the speaker to promote the superiority of one thing over the other.

It is the recognition and sharing of the similarities of parts or features of two items that lead to three ways comparison may be used in speeches: (1) to explain complex ideas and processes; (2) to explain common experiences in a new way; (3) to assist audiences in making choices. There are many more possible ways that a speaker can use the tool of comparison as the frame for a whole speech or as a support material in a speech that incorporates a different organizational structure. The three above are probably the most common. We will look again at comparison as a speech technique when we get to argument speeches and study specific argument patterns that depend on comparison.

Speeches to Explain Complex Ideas and Processes

One of the most valuable outcomes of using the support material of comparison in speeches is to help audiences understand abstract, difficult, or distant material. These speeches depend on the close resemblance of the parts of the two things being compared. Such comparative explanations are often in the form called **analogies**. Analogies focus on how the parts are similar. You may remember some analogies teachers have used in the past to explain difficult concepts. If the comparisons were well conceived, you probably not only gained new understanding, but also remember the component parts of the concept because you had a familiar base to hang them on.

Comparisons that have the primary purpose of explaining or clarifying unfamiliar and complex material should have three characteristics. (1) The speaker methodically explains each part of the concept or object by telling how each part or feature of one is like the other. (2) The comparison item that is being used to explain or clarify should be (a) more concrete, (b) on a smaller scale, (c) more simple, or (d) physically closer to the audience. For example, to understand the magnitude of the Great Wall of China, a speaker

could compare it to a wall of Lego blocks built through the city and state where the speech is being given. (3) The audience should already be very familiar with one item of the pair used in the comparison. In the previous example comparing pipes and arteries, it is assumed that audiences have had more close-up experience with pipes than they have with human arteries.

Below is an example of an analogy for promoting understanding and learning. The explanation of "pulse laser light" exemplifies the three characteristics of a good analogy. The author Richard Arthur uses step-by-step comparisons of the features of pulse laser light and a marching band. The band, of course, is more concrete, observable, and familiar to the audience members. By comparing the movement characteristics of the band with the characteristics of a new phenomenon to the audience, pulse laser light, audience members should be able to use the mental pictures of the characteristics of moving people to help them visualize and remember the characteristics of pulse laser light.

Notice that this excerpt contains two pairs of comparisons: Same Class Comparison of pulse laser light with ordinary light, and marching bands with mobs; and Different Class Comparisons of pulse laser light with a marching band and ordinary light with mobs.

The Engineer's Guide to Better Communication
by Richard H. Arthur

> Pulse laser light is different from ordinary light in the same way a marching group of people is different from a disorganized mob. A mob moves randomly, moving in all directions at the same time. This is like the motion of ordinary light, where the particles of light, called photons, move in all directions at the same time. In a marching group, the people move in the same direction. Laser light is like this, all its photons move in the same direction at the same time. In a mob, all the people move at different speeds, which is like the

different frequencies in ordinary light. The different frequencies, or colors of light, are randomly distributed, and vibrate at different speeds. Laser light is all one color, vibrating at the same speed. The people in a marching group all move at the same speed.

Not only do they move at the same speed, but the people moving in a marching group also move in step. Each person moves his right foot at the same time as all the others, and does the same with his left. Laser light is like that also, all its photons move in phase, with all the photons reaching the peak of their vibrations at the same time. The lowest point, like the point in a step where the legs are side by side, is also reached at the same time. In ordinary light, even if the light was monochrome light, all one color, and sent out in a spotlight beam, it would not yet be laser light, as the photons would not be in phase. This can be explained as even if a mob were to voluntarily move in one direction, at the same time, at the same speed, it would not be a marching group. The marching group has a precision that comes from its discipline and training that a mob would never have.

Laser light is more concentrated and intense than ordinary light, because all its photons deliver their energy at the same time, in the same way a marching group will arrive, all together, at its destination.

Speeches to Explain Common Experiences in a New Way

This second type of speech also emphasizes how the characteristics of two things are alike; however, here the Audience Outcome Goal is different. A speaker who uses comparison to provide audiences with insight into common experiences will probably be aiming for both cognitive and affective changes. Consequently, some of the characteristics of these speeches also differ from those in which the speaker primarily wants to explain difficult material. In a speech to explain common experiences in a new way, (1) the speaker again points out, in an organized fashion, the similarities of the individual characteristics of the two items being compared, (2) both of the items in the pair are familiar to the audience, and (3) the two items are not usually thought of together. It is the new revelations that come from the juxtaposition of an unexpected pair that gives these speeches their power to help the audience gain new understanding of something that is a common part of their lives.

Here are some examples of speech topics students have used for speeches to give audiences new understanding about common experiences: (a) choosing friends is like choosing soda; (b) a child is like a river; (c) skipping class is like being an alcoholic; and (d) a pair of shoes is like a relationship.

This speech is a popular approach to comparison because it allows the speaker to show creativity, and audiences find these speeches interesting and entertaining. However, many speeches for enlightenment fall flat because the speaker does not really expand the consciousness of the audience on the topic, but merely points out what is already obvious to everyone. A good speech of this type requires hard, original thinking. A cute topic that worked for a friend last semester may not work for you unless you develop the topic in a new and unique way that is completely based on your own understanding and ideas.

Speeches to Assist in Making a Choice

The characteristics of speeches designed to help audiences make choices are: (1) the comparison focuses on similar features that the speaker methodically compares so that the audience can learn which is the superior choice; (2) differences are based on degree (such as size, cost, quality, efficiency, number of benefits) of features; (3) Same Class Comparisons are used.

The first two types of comparative speech approaches we have discussed have informative or entertainment purposes. Speeches that help an audience to make a choice may have either an informative or persuasive intent, depending on whether the speaker takes an advocacy position or not. A speaker or writer may take an unbiased view and simply provide information about the characteristics of the two things being compared in order to provide greater understanding about both that will be useful in decision-making. For example, an ink jet and a laser printer might be compared on such issues as cost, size, quality of printing, and versatility. The communicator is not advocating that one is better than the other, but is attempting to increase audience knowledge and information about the two.

When speakers decide to openly support the superiority of one of the pair over the other, they still use the basic organizational plan of presenting the features of the two competing products or ideas to the audience. However, in this case, the speaker selects the most relevant or advantageous characteristics of the two elements being compared and lines them up against one another clearly advocating one choice over the other. For example, the speaker illustrates the advantages of cost, size, quality of print, and versatility for one printer over the other and leads the audience to the inevitable conclusion that whichever printer the speaker is supporting is best.

An alternative method for helping the audience to arrive at a conclusion about which of a pair is the best choice is to set up criteria against which each recommendation is tested. The speaker decides which are the most relevant features for decision-making, shows which proposal best matches the criteria, and leads the audience toward making a choice based on comparison.

ACTIVITY **8.1**
Three Types of Comparison Speeches

Instructors may assign this activity for group work or individual work.

Part I: Choose one of the topics below and create a brief comparison to explain the topic to an audience.

- Explain the differences between high and low pressures in weather patterns.

- Explain the relationship between inflation and interest rates.

- Explain the concept of "entropy."

- Explain how the human body "fights" infection.

- Explain the disorder of dyslexia.

_____

_____

_____

_____

Part II: Choose one of the topics below and create a brief comparison to explain a common experience in a new way.

- What it's like to finish college and move into the next phase of life.

- The differences between masculine and feminine worldviews.

- The life of a "fast food employee."

- Learning to play a musical instrument.

- The political and leadership styles of (either George W. Bush or Barack Obama).

_____

_____

_____

_____

Part III. List three sets of objects or ideas you can compare so that the audience would have a basis on which to make a choice between the two.

1. _____

2. _____

3. _____

■ Building a Comparison Speech: Global Decisions

Topic Selection

As you have been reading about the three types of comparison speeches, you may have started to make tentative decisions about which type you would like to use and what topic you will speak about. Students often find this assignment difficult to get started on because they go about it from the wrong direction. When starting to look for a topic for the comparison speech assignment a student should not first ask, "What are two things I can compare?" A better approach is to begin by coming up with a subject you want to explain to the audience or a proposition you want to convince the audience to accept. Find a topic that you know and care about that fulfills the need to know for an audience, then ask "How can I use comparison to help the audience understand, or how can I use comparison to persuade my audience?"

When students merely look for two things to compare, they may end up with a topic that has little or no value for either the speaker or the audience. Not only does the general subject have to be worthwhile, there also has to be a good reason to make the comparison. There is no point in telling the audience that high school and college are alike in some ways. The general subject of secondary and higher education may be valuable and relevant to an audience, but since your audience already knows the similarities of the two levels of education, a comparison does not serve any useful or interesting purpose. Following the process given below should lead to a topic appropriate for a comparison speech.

Topic Selection Process for Comparison Speech

1. Start with surveying your own specialized knowledge. See if there is some difficult, complex, or new subject area in which you have expertise. Alternatively, look for a current issue or new product you are interested in or know about.

2. Determine if the subject you now have in mind is something that would be worthwhile for your audience to learn about. If you have found a topic that will provide your audience with new information or understanding, and has personal or societal relevance, then you are ready to move on to checking the topic against the assignment.

3. Can you find a comparison approach that will be useful in presenting the topic to the audience? Look at the characteristics for the three speech approaches to determine which fits your topic best. One way to do this is by checking the type of information you want to present—complex, remote, common experiences, or controversial.

4. Can you find an appropriate object, idea, process to compare your topic to?

Most students find that using the above approaches will help them find a solid relevant topic that fits the assignment.

Additional Global Decisions

At this point you have a topic and have no doubt already started to think about how you will develop the speech. You may have already decided on *Audience Outcome Goals* (AOG). Be sure to write the goal or goals down on the Speech Planning Sheet. This will help you to discover secondary goals you may not have originally included and keep you focused on the audience as you move on with the speech construction. As has already been pointed out, most comparison speeches have either cognitive or affective goals; however, some speeches might have behavioral goals as secondary goals.

By now you should be ready to write a tentative **Thesis Statement** and decide on the **Main Points.** Remember to include both the narrowed topic and a statement of how the speech will be developed in your Thesis Statement. Below are some examples of Thesis Statements for the three types of Comparison Speeches.

Speeches to Explain Complex Ideas and Processes

* **Thesis**: Pulse laser light can be explained by comparing it to the movements of a marching band in three ways: (a) direction; (b) speed; (c) synchronization.

Speeches to Explain Common Experiences in a New Way

* **Thesis**: Being in college is like being in jail in four ways: (a) living accommodations; (b) type of work; (c) length of sentence; and (d) hope of release.

Speeches to Aid in Making a Choice

* **Thesis**: An analysis of the Plus/Minus System of grading is based on comparing a university without plus/minus grades and a university with plus/minus grades on three issues: (a) how the grades impact students' GPA; (b) how accurately the grades reflect student achievement; and (c) how popular each system is throughout the nation.

* **Thesis**: A bicycle is superior to a moped based on three factors: (a) cost, (b) exercise, and (c) impact on the environment.

* **Thesis**: The U.S. should adopt a health care program like that of Canada in order to gain the benefits experienced in Canada: (a) better health for all citizens; (b) fairer distribution of the cost of health care; and (c) cost savings based on early treatment.

Organizing Main Points for a Comparison Speech

While writing your tentative Thesis Statement, you have already made some decision about your Main Points. For most comparison speeches, regardless of whether the intention is to promote learning or to persuade, the Main Points will be related to the component characteristics of the comparison pair. Rudolf Verderber in the book *Essentials of Informative Speaking** presents two logical ways to organize the parts or features of the two things being compared. The first of these is the **Divided Pattern**, where you name the two things being compared and then list all the features or criteria for one thing and then for the other. The second is the **Alternating Pattern**, where you show how each compatible feature compares to the other thing (you may list each criteria first).

---

* Published by Wadsworth Publishing, 1991.

An outline for the body of each type of organizational pattern might look like this:

General Model

Divided	Alternating
I. Thing 1	I. Feature 1
A. Feature 1	A. Thing 1
B. Feature 2	B. Thing 2
C. Feature 3	II. Feature 2
II. Thing 2	A. Thing 1
A. Feature 1	B. Thing 2
B. Feature 2	III. Feature 3
C. Feature 3	A. Thing 1
	B. Thing 2

Specific Example

Thesis: "Ferarris are better than Hondas based on two features."

Divided	Alternating
I. Ferarris	I. Speed
A. Speed	A. Ferarris
B. Acceleration	B. Hondas
II. Hondas	II. Acceleration
A. Speed	A. Ferarris
B. Acceleration	B. Hondas

This specific example represents a speech for making a **choice**. In this case the speaker has decided to attempt to persuade the audience toward the speaker's viewpoint. The same organization however could be used with a different Thesis and Conclusion if the speaker wished to present an unbiased comparison of the two cars.

The following outline uses the Alternating Pattern.

Thesis: "If you enjoy reading fantasy, you will also enjoy reading science fiction because of the similarity of essential features."

Main Points:

I. Fantasy and Science Fiction both employ unusual setting.

    A. Fantasy generally takes place in mystic lands.

    B. Science Fiction generally takes place on other worlds.

II. Fantasy and Science Fiction both employ unusual tools.

    A. Fantasy generally involves magical powers.

    B. Science fiction generally involves fantastic technology.

III. *(etc., etc.)*

In this example, the speaker's goal is to help the audience appreciate science fiction by **explaining science fiction in a new way** as audience members are introduced to the similarities the genre shares with fantasy literature. When a speaker wishes to create a speech for explaining **complex ideas or processes**, this same example may be used.

---

* The examples in this section were created by Robert McMasters, a GTA at Kansas State 1991–1993.

ACTIVITY **8.2**
Organizing Main Points

Write two brief topic outlines for the comparison of pulse laser light to a marching band seen earlier in the chapter. First write an outline using the Divided Pattern. Then for the same comparison, write an outline using the Alternating Pattern.

Divided Pattern

Alternating Pattern

■ Building a Comparison Speech: Local Decisions

Selection of Items for Comparison

When choosing the topic for the speech, the author makes tentative decisions about just what will be compared in the speech. Before the development of the speech progresses very far, it is wise to test to make sure the selected items are appropriate for a successful comparison speech. Here are five guidelines to use in testing the two things you plan to compare.

Testing Comparison Items

1. **The two items being compared must have significant similarities**. Comparisons are weak when only a few minor features naturally overlap and the communicator must stretch to make the comparison fit. Concentrating on all the ways the two are dissimilar will distract audiences. "Life is probably not like a chocolate chip cookie."

2. When using comparison to explain something difficult or unfamiliar, **the other element must be already familiar to the audience**. Usually the familiar item is also more immediate to the audience and simpler in nature. Do not ask the audience to have to learn about the first element in order to teach them about the second element.

3. When advocating the superiority of one of the pair over the other, **speakers must be sure they can legitimately support the claimed superiority of the chosen situation**. It is dangerous to ask the audience to compare two relatively equal proposals. The speaker may even have to admit some benefits from the alternative solutions. The speaker must be able to either refute those alleged benefits, minimize their impact, or overwhelm other contribution with a multitude of benefits from the preferred solution.

4. A communicator must use a series of comparison, but **it is better not to intermix different comparisons in a short space of time, especially within one sentence**. Mixed metaphors or any rapid changes from one comparison to another are not evil, just untidy and a little confusing.

5. **Try to make comparisons new and fresh**. Novelty not only increases audience curiosity and immediate interest, but encourages the audience to work through the comparison with the speaker. Both audience interest and participation improve chances of the audience remembering the comparison and what they gained from it.

Comparative Language

You use comparative language daily, usually almost unconsciously. We use metaphors (communication theorists use the term "metaphor" to refer to all forms of comparative language) to tell how we feel. "You make me sick." "I'm on top of the world." "This is as exciting as watching Astro Turf grow."

Comparative language is commonly used to condense or simplify complex ideas or plans, such as political programs. In the tradition of President Franklin Roosevelt's "New Deal" and President Lyndon Johnson's "Great Society," more recently the Republican Party has offered the metaphoric label "Contract With America." Often people don't consciously think about what the term means. We just respond to the general positive nature of the term. "Contracts" are good things. They usually mean work, salary increases, and that we have had a say in our future. The details of any political program are extensive and controversial. It's easier to talk about and convince people about a political proposal by using a comforting metaphoric title.

Almost any speech is improved through the use of comparative language because it works so well to carry emotional messages and because it distills abstract or complex concepts. According to communication scholars George Lakoff and Mark Johnson in their book, *Metaphors We Live By*, metaphoric language not only reveals how the speaker feels and what the speaker believes, but also shapes the user's and audience's values, attitudes, emotions, and even patterns of thought.

The following example illustrates the relationship of metaphoric language and changing beliefs.

For many years, people referred to the United States as a "melting pot."

This metaphor was used proudly to tell the world that when people from different countries came to America, they would have their home culture, practices, and traditions all melted away and they would emerge as new beings with new American language, beliefs, and behaviors. Recently, this metaphor has become unacceptable to many people because for them it represents a loss. Instead they want to substitute a new metaphor such as:

"America is a salad" (all individual vegetables are still identifiable but have a common dressing).

---

or

"America is a stew" (the meat and vegetables are separate, but the gravy is held in common).

The movement to change the melting pot metaphor is based on the belief that metaphors can change how people think, believe, and act about something, in this case a multicultural society.

Part of the power of metaphor comes from the active role of receiver in decoding the metaphoric symbol that has been chosen to represent something that may be quite different. Usually the two

items are from different classes and the speaker does not explain to the audience how the parts of the two are alike, but leaves that interpretation up to the audience. For example, if someone tells you, "the enrollment process is a nightmare," you automatically know the person is making a comparison (you don't have to go to sleep and dream to enroll) and that the most obvious and potent characteristics of nightmares (a bad experience, a feeling of helplessness) also apply to the enrollment process.

In a Comparison Speech, comparative language can help to reinforce the primary comparison defined in the thesis. Especially for a Comparison Speech, the speaker should give careful attention to wording the Main Points. This is an excellent opportunity to choose metaphoric labels for the primary ideas you want to emphasize.

In addition to using comparative language in the frame of the speech, you may want to try to use an **ongoing metaphor**, a series of metaphoric phrases or words included throughout the speech that are derived from the same basic metaphor. Here is an example of an **ongoing metaphor** used by Jean Haley in a *Kansas City Star* article published in February 1994, approximately six months after the devastating Midwest flood of 1993. The overarching metaphor is a comparison of flood victims in the post-flood months to close family and friends in the period of mourning after a funeral.

The ritual of public mourning is over. The relatives returned home. All the home-cooked food brought by solicitous neighbors has been eaten. Then reality sets in. Just when grief is the loneliest and need for support peaks, no one stops by to give comfort.

In this example, the writer has moved well beyond just surface similarities. Through the series of metaphors, the author has started to build the pattern of comparison of the parts for the receivers. This example illustrates the role the audience must play in making meaning out of comparative language. In spite of the author's help, the receivers still have considerable work to do. They must make their own connections. The "ritual of public mourning" for the death may be compared to the furor of media coverage of the flood and flood victims. The "relatives who returned home" are like the out-of-state volunteers who filled sandbags, served sandwiches, and sent relief goods. Receiver completes the comparison for each of the parts based on their own backgrounds and understanding.

Not all ongoing metaphors specifically present the parts of the main metaphor as obviously as this one does. The speaker or writer may choose an overall metaphor that subtly reappears over and over in the weave of the speech as the communicator repeats threads and recombines colors through the words and images. Many political speakers use a "war" metaphor to influence attitudes related to a social problem such as poverty or drug use. The speaker will talk about "fighting" against problems, trying to win, recommend "weapons," admit there may be "losses." Notice that these metaphors are not limited to nouns but include verbs such as "fighting" and "win." The audience may not even be aware of a speaker's metaphor at a conscious level, but the gradual build and repetition of the design will influence both understanding and conviction of audience members.

Completing the Comparison Speech

By this point, your basic plan of the comparison speech is complete. Now go back and create the introduction and conclusion. Be sure to share with the audience the significance of the speech subject for them. The introduction and conclusion are good places to use comparative language that contributes to the overall effectiveness of the speech. The following is a brief outline of a speech designed to explain a **complex concept**.

*Brief Outline Designed to Explain a Complex Speech**

Introduction

I.   (*Opener*) Did you ever stop to think about how that computer you use everyday actually works.

II. (*Intro-transition*) Computers play a tremendous role in today's society, so it's important that we know at least a little bit about them.

III. (*Thesis and Preview*) A personal computer functions much like the human brain. Each has input, output, memory, and processing capabilities.

Body

I.   Both the brain and the computer have input.

    A. The keyboard is like our sense of hearing.

    B. Scanners are like our sense of sight.

    C. Other devices are like our other senses.

II. Both the brain and the computer have output.

    A. The audio/video output is like speaking to someone.

    B. The printer is like writing something down.

III. Both the brain and the computer have memory.

    A. Computer ROMS are like long-term memory.

    B. Computer RAMS are like short-term memory.

IV. Both the brain and the computer have processing capabilities.

    A. Computer IC chips are like brain neurons.

Conclusion:

I.   As you can see, personal computers work in a way similar to our own brains through input, output, memory, and processing capabilities.

II. The next time you sit down and type up a speech, remember that it takes just as much work for your computer as it did for you.

---

* Sample outline was created by Robert McMasters, GTA, Kansas State

ACTIVITY **8.3**
Identifying Comparison Concepts

The contemporary author, William Least Heat-Moon is a master at comparison. In this excerpt from his book *PrairyErth*, almost every sentence contains at least one comparison.

As you read, mark each example of comparison you find.

PrairyErth

Underneath eastern Kansas lies a range, the Nemaha Mountains, and just now I am walking up what would be the foothills of its steep eastern face. I'm near the western edge of Fox Creek quadrangle and following a ridge track above Gannon branch that I hope will lead to an oil well, this one a dry hole drilled years ago. In my pack is a hefty wrench that I plan to use to uncap the pipe and open a little window, a porthole, onto the old buried mountains, ones from the time of the Ozarks and the Black Hills. When the Rockies were still prostrate, one theory holds, the Nemahas rose and then eroded as the Appalachians reared up to relieve the crustal pressure, the birth of one being the death of the other.

In Chase County, of the nearly four hundred gas and oil wells drilled, only a couple of dozen reached the Precambrian rock of the Nemaha Ridge, the crest today six hundred feet below sea level and much eroded from what it once was. A Kansas geologist a half century ago said the Nemahas *must have been originally one of the great ranges of mountains of the earth*. With their nearly vertical eastern flank and their much less precipitous western exposure, I imagine them in their first days looking like the Tetons.

In front of you imagine on the floor a thick book, like an encyclopedia, and atop it seven slender books; push the books to your left so they slide down to overlap like shingles on a roof: the encyclopedia is the Precambrian crystalline core, here thrust up into a mountainous fold, and the books atop it are the seven periods of the Paleozoic era that describe Chase County; all of this is to say that on top of the antediluvian granite rest the marine-made layers of sedimentary rock, mostly successions of shale and limestone, old sea floors that have since been slightly tilted. The leaves of these volumes of rock are the individual strata that compose the county, here rubble-strewn, there fertile, arable here, only grazable there. Once, probably, three additional volumes lay atop this slipped stack, but water and wind have sent them eastward.

The uppermost of the seven books represents fifty million years of sediments settling to the bottom of a sea that came and left again and again like a quarreling lover. The history here is this: a sea transgressing, regressing, transgressing, in and out, up and down, higher, lower, always advancing, withdrawing always, and always leaving something behind, the sea conceiving stone, and the rock bearing living things that turn mineral solutions—calcium carbonates—into shell and bone, and bone becoming stone again, and that too waiting to become again; and everywhere cycles, and cycles within cycles, and the sea laying down strata like shrouds over the old life, and then the corrupting winds and waters coming to resurrect it. The Nemahas rose, were partly eroded, subsided, and were buried, all of this happening in the Eastern Hemisphere; and then, slowly and passively like a casket, the range got carried into the Western world to come here—to what appears a permanent resting place—where the thirty-eighth parallel crosses the ninety-sixth meridian; so, in this way, Chase County, Kansas, migrated from the far other side just as its human inhabitants were to do. In the half century since I was born, this hill has moved at about the rate a fingernail grows, some four feet farther west—about the distance from my heel to my hip—as has everything else around it, the Cottonwood, the courthouse, the brass bedsteads.

Answer the following questions about the reading from *PrairyErth*.

1. How many examples of comparison did you underline? _____

   _____

2. Which of the three types of comparison speeches does the comparison of the layers of rock to books best fit?

   _____

3. Which type of organizational pattern has the author used in the section comparing layers of rocks and books, divided or alternating?

   _____

4. Give one example from the reading of Same Class Comparison.

   _____

5. Give one example from the reading of Different Class Comparison.

   _____

6. Identify an ongoing metaphor used in the reading. Give specific examples of the language used in the ongoing metaphor you selected.

   _____

7. What did you think was the most effect example of comparison from the reading?

   _____

■ Key Concepts

Below are some key concepts from this chapter. Test yourself by seeing if you can explain each of the concepts.

- same class comparison

- different class comparison

- types of comparison speeches

- topic selection

- organizational patterns for comparison speeches

- comparative language

- choosing comparison items

Chapter Study Guide
You should be able to:
• Define "Comparison" and explain the two types of *focus* or *viewpoint levels* used to consider similarities between two things.
• Explain and give examples of *Same Class Comparisons* and *Different Class Comparisons*.
• Tell the differences between each of the following and give an example of each: (1) speech to explain complex ideas and processes, (2) speech to explain common experiences in a new way, and (3) speech to assist in making a choice.
• Give guidelines for selecting a topic for a comparison speech.
• Write thesis statements for the three types of comparison speeches.
• Differentiate between and give examples of *Divided Pattern* and *Alternating Pattern*.
• Give guidelines for testing the fit of comparison items.
• List three functions of comparative language.
• Explain and give an example of an ongoing metaphor.

ASSIGNMENT
Comparison

Length: Between 3 and 5 minutes

Task: Speaker will present a comparison using one of the following categories:

  1. speech to explain complex ideas or processes,

  2. speech to explain common experiences in a new way,

  3. speech to aid in making a choice.

Oral presentation will include introduction, development of comparison, and conclusion. All parts of a full introduction and conclusion should be present. Internal transitions should be included between Main Points in the speech body. The speaker must use comparative language in addition to developing the primary comparison. The speaker must use and cite one outside source of information.

Note restrictions: You may use one 4 × 6 notecard if you wish to. You are not required to use any notes; however you are required to hand in either the notecard or a brief outline or map of the plan of the speech at the end of the speech.

Preparation: Fill out and turn in the "Speech Planning Sheet." In addition, you should practice and time the presentation as you plan to present it in class.

Speech Planning Sheet

1. What is the Audience Outcome Goal?

   _____

   _____

2. What is the Thesis being developed in the speech?

   _____

   _____

3. Which type of Comparison Speech are you using?

   _____

   _____

4. Which additional comparative language are you using?

   _____

   _____

5. What is the significance of the topic of comparison for the audience?

   _____

   _____

6. What outside source(s) did you use as research to support the comparison?

   _____

   _____

7. How long was the speech in the final practice? _____ minutes

Sample Speech Planning Sheet

1. What is the Audience Outcome Goal?

    To understand the role of tectonic plate movements in earth disruptions (earthquakes,

    volcanoes, tsunamis).

2. What is the Thesis being developed in the speech?

    The movements that result in (1) separation, (2) collision, (3) sliding and locking of

    tectonic plates resting on magma and carrying continents are like the movements

    and collisions of crackers on Jell-O carrying peanut butter.

3. Which type of Comparison Speech are you using?

    Explaining Complex Ideas and Processes.

4. Which additional comparative language are you using?

5. What is the significance of the topic of comparison for the audience?

    Large numbers of shocks (and quakes each year; part of the fear of quakes is based on a

    lack of knowledge about why quakes occur and how the location of quakes can be predicted).

6. What outside source(s) did you use as research to support the comparison?

    "Earthquake" by L. Don Leet in Encyclopedia American, 1995.

    Published by Grolier Incorporated, Danbury, Connecticut.

7. How long was the speech in the final practice? __4 ½__ minutes

■ Sample Notecard

Introduction:

Opener: *Mystic belief of North American Indians that earthquakes result from movements of giant tortoise that carried the earth on its back.*

Significance for Audience: *Combination of quakes and shocks ranging from destructive shocks to minor shocks equals over a million a year; need knowledge of quake causes to reduce fear and confusion.*

Thesis (and Preview): *I will explain the three most common ways that crustal plates move and collide to cause earth disruptions. First, some plates move apart and separate; second, plates move toward each other and collide; third, plates slide along each other.*

Body (Development):

Movement apart showing strain on Jell-O that results in openings for volcanic material
Movement together showing one cracker riding up on another or both crumbling
Move side-by-side showing stress of lock and crumbling of cracker when released

Summary and Conclusion:

Remember that when tectonic plates pull apart, collide together, and slide past each other, earth disturbances occur because the Jell-O pulls apart and becomes thin, one cracker may ride over the other, and the stress of movements may cause crackers to break; crumble and become displaced.

Instructor's Evaluation of Comparison

Speaker aroused curiosity, prepared audience during opener _____

Speaker established an appropriate audience "need to know" _____

Speaker clearly shared Thesis and preview of Main Points _____

Thesis and Main Points are mutually inclusive _____

Speaker selected effective comparison strategies consistent with the speech goal _____

Relationship between pair was appropriate (same class, different class, familiar–unfamiliar, essential similarities, supported superiority) _____

Speaker avoided trite comparisons _____

Speaker used comparative language in addition to primary comparison _____

Speaker cited outside sources _____

Speaker maintained audience interest _____

Speaker presented obvious transitions between Main Points in body _____

Speaker summarized main points _____

Speaker chose a closing that was consistent with and reinforced the Thesis and Audience Outcome _____

Speech moved toward realization of Audience Outcome Goal (understanding, appreciation, entertainment, persuasion) _____

Speaker maintained a natural, conversational delivery style _____

Speaker used voice and body to increase understanding and interest _____

Speaker refrained from distracting voice and body behaviors _____

Speaker maintained eye contact _____

Speaker projected confidence _____

Instructor's Evaluation of Comparison

Speaker aroused curiosity, prepared audience during opener　　　_____

Speaker established an appropriate audience "need to know"　　　_____

Speaker clearly shared Thesis and preview of Main Points　　　_____

Thesis and Main Points are mutually inclusive　　　_____

Speaker selected effective comparison strategies consistent
with the speech goal　　　_____

Relationship between pair was appropriate (same class,
different class, familiar–unfamiliar, essential similarities,
supported superiority)　　　_____

Speaker avoided trite comparisons　　　_____

Speaker used comparative language in addition to primary
comparison　　　_____

Speaker cited outside sources　　　_____

Speaker maintained audience interest　　　_____

Speaker presented obvious transitions between Main Points
in body　　　_____

Speaker summarized main points　　　_____

Speaker chose a closing that was consistent with and reinforced
the Thesis and Audience Outcome　　　_____

Speech moved toward realization of Audience Outcome Goal
(understanding, appreciation, entertainment, persuasion)　　　_____

Speaker maintained a natural, conversational delivery style　　　_____

Speaker used voice and body to increase understanding and
interest　　　_____

Speaker refrained from distracting voice and body behaviors　　　_____

Speaker maintained eye contact　　　_____

Speaker projected confidence　　　_____

Peer Evaluation of Comparison

Name of Speaker _____   Your Name _____

Speech Topic _____

Listening for Content

1. What did you think was the Thesis of the speech? _____

   _____

2. What did you think was the Audience Outcome Goal? _____

   _____

3. What did you think were the Main Points? _____

   _____

4. How did the speaker establish audience "need to know"? _____

   _____

5. Which type of Comparison Speech did the speaker use? _____

   _____

Listening for Evaluation

1. What comparison did you think was most effective and why? _____

   _____

2. What delivery aspect (how the speaker looked and sounded) was most effective and why? _____

   _____

3. Name two things that would have improved the speech. _____

   _____

CHAPTER 9
Memorization

Chapter Objectives
After reading the chapter you should be able to:
• Identify general attributes of good speech building that promote memory of the speech and its content.
• Discuss the roles of the following memory variables: (a) motivation, (b) nature of the information, (c) creating meaning and associations, and (d) repetition.
• Enumerate speech strategies that promote memory.

Chapter Overview

We have emphasized *remembering* as one of the Audience Outcome Goals in earlier sections of the text. In this section, we will introduce and explain the special strategies the speaker can incorporate in speeches to promote audience retention and recall of a speech. There are two different categories of speech building decisions that help an audience remember a speech and its content: (1) decisions that produce an organized, interesting speech and (2) decisions that increase the memory potential of specific information.

Several general attributes of effective speeches aid indirectly in promoting memory such as (1) content and delivery elements that capture and maintain audience attention, (2) a logical plan of speech structure that is shared with the audience,

and (3) clear explanations and arguments that the audience understands. In other words, when the speechmaker has maximized audience attention, participation, and understanding, the speaker has also increased the probability that the audience will remember the speech.

Memory-Enhancing Variables

Before we explore specific memory-enhancing speech strategies, it is helpful to first look at some of the common factors that increase retention of specific information for most people. These memory-enhancing variables form the basis for the speaker strategies.

Think about the mountain of information you are exposed to in just one day. You are bombarded nonstop by sensory data every minute; however, only a small fraction of what you see and hear ends up in long-term memory. You automatically filter and select what you will keep and what will be discarded. You can probably identify some of the variables that determine why one experience will be forever engraved in your memory and another will be forgotten immediately.

No doubt some of the memory variables you are already aware of are included in the following four **Memory-enhancing Variables**: (1) motivations to remember information; (2) the nature of the information to be remembered; (3) the understanding of the meaning and relationship of the information; and (4) repetition and rehearsal of the information.

Motivation to Remember

When remembering requires effort, we may be motivated to memorize because we will be rewarded if we can remember and punished if we cannot. Rewards are conventionally divided into (1) extrinsic and (2) intrinsic rewards. Extrinsic rewards come from another person or agent and include material rewards such as cupcakes, money, trophies, prizes (THE CAR!) and non-material rewards such as praise, prestige, grades, and power. Intrinsic rewards come from yourself and include self-satisfaction, increased self-esteem, and greater personal independence.

All of us memorize a great many facts that we perceive will be useful to us. We are rewarded by saving time, getting high test scores, and impressing others. When we can't remember, we may be punished by the frustration of having to go search for information we have forgotten or even worse be powerless when we lack vital information at a time when split-seconds count.

Nature of the Information

Even when strong motivations to commit information to memory are present, it is clear that not all facts are equally easy to memorize. Whether you find it easy or difficult to remember an event or information may depend on the nature of the content itself.

Experiences that are *vivid, dramatic, or vital* are easier to remember than those that lack these characteristics. These three adjectives are certainly not synonyms, but the experiences they describe are apt to have common elements. These are events which have a high sensory and/or emotional content. The term "vital" is used here to refer to that which is important to "life." This includes those experiences that are dangerous, even life-threatening, as well as those that support the prolongation of life and well-being.

Almost the opposite of this category of high intensity content is a second category based on lightweight experiences. This set of "easy memories" are often *humorous or novel*. We may remember these kinds of experiences because of the pleasure connected with the experiences. Closely related to information we remember because it is new or unique are those nuggets of data we tuck away because they are so bizarre or outrageous that we just can't forget them.

Probably the most difficult materials to memorize are *pieces of information that lack meaning for the learner*. Abstract language, new symbols, gobbledygook, and nonsense syllables just zip right past unless someone makes it meaningful. There is reduced probability this information will be retained when confusing or meaningless information also seems to be dry and sterile, unless the learner works very hard to etch the record of that information into his or her brain.

Creating Meaning and Associations

Obviously learners are able to master information that is difficult to memorize. If the problem is based in the confusing nature of the content, a logical first step is to attempt to change the nature of the information from meaningless to meaningful through **Explanation**. The explanation can come from either outside sources such as books or teachers or the learner may be able to grapple with the information and make sense of the data through personal mental efforts. Once an information receiver understands what has formerly been only vague signals, then the new comprehensible nature of the content will promote retention.

A second information processing phenomenon that increases the likelihood of remembering is building **Associations** between the new information and previously learned information. Part of understanding meaning is understanding where new data fits into the schemes of data a person already has in memory. From the time you were a very young child, you started to create patterns of information in your memory. We each build our own specific connections as new information comes to us, yet probably all students in your class in a general way have similar metaphorical file folders in their memory. An example of such a centralized information file would be a folder labeled "winter clothes." When each of us first encountered "mittens," we *associated* them with other items in the winter clothes category such as jackets and hats and because of the association, "mittens" ended up in the "winter clothes" folder. The association with a general category, and with specific similar data, helped us remember "mittens."

These placement associations are usually logical (oh, now I understand; a "gnatcatcher" is a small New World bird with gray and white plumage and a long tail. It fits in the file folder in my brain labeled "Small Birds"). Other powerful associations work because they are absurdly illogical (I picture a small bird wearing a baseball glove ready to catch a gnat).

Repetition of Information

Repeated bombardment of the senses with images, sounds, or other sensory signals usually leads to memorization. If you see, hear, say, or move a set of muscles in a repetitive pattern, you will probably commit the experience to memory. Some senses seem to be more effective for some individuals than others. You may learn to spell words by writing the words over and over. Your brother may learn best by saying the letters of the words over and over out loud.

Most people benefit by experiencing the information through multiple senses. Learners remember more when they experience the information through sight, hearing, and touch. These sensory exposures may occur simultaneously or independently. In either case, the result is repeated exposure to the same data.

■ Specific Speech Strategies to Promote Memory

Obviously, speakers can implement strategies that utilize these natural memory assisting factors.

1. *Introduce both extrinsic and intrinsic motivations to memorize.* You can offer rewards, either material or non-material, and/or punishments as extrinsic motivations. "Anyone who gets all the answers correct on the 5-question quiz, will get a package of "Smarties" candies; anyone who gets four or fewer correct, gets a "Dum-dum." It is generally recommended that speakers emphasize reward rather than punishment. However, it is a common strategy (at least by teachers) to remind audience members of the consequences of not learning something. In this case, the speaker may not be the agent who metes out the punishment but merely the messenger who gives the warning about potential punishment.

2. *Choose vivid language that emphasizes the dramatic and/or vital nature of what is to be learned.* Language that is concrete, specific, and related to the senses or emotions increases the dramatic impression the communication makes on the mind of the listener and also makes the content more meaningful. Explicitly pointing out the vital nature of the content adds drama (a matter of life and death!) and personal meaning. Specific, concrete words call up pictures in our minds so that we have a visual association with what we are to learn. A mental picture of a black and white cow is easier to store away than the phrase "domesticated quadruped."

3. *Use humor or entertaining strategies.* Don't let the humor overwhelm what you want the audience to learn. If you do, the audience may just remember that something was funny and why it was funny, but forget the content they were to learn.

4. *Make the content meaningful.* Understanding must come first. Clarify the content that is to be learned. It is helpful to the audience to attach personal meaning to the content. If they understand cognitively, and also understand the application of the content, the odds in favor of memorizing go up.

5. *Point out and/or create associations.* Part of understanding may be the recognition of where this new content will fit in the larger scheme of information. How does this relate to what we have already learned or will learn in the near future? Many learning tricks such as mnemonic devices are based on association. Students memorize the names of the planets in order from the sun outward by learning a sentence totally unrelated to astronomy: "Mother Visits Every Morning, Just Stays Until Noon Period." Remembering the first letter of each word in the statement reminds students of Mercury, Venus, Earth, Mars, Jupiter, Saturn, Uranus, Neptune and Pluto. An alternate sentence may have even more direct association. "My Very Educated Mother Just Served Us Nine Pizzas." Since the learner has to memorize both the aid and the information related to it, humorous or absurd memory aids are a good choice. You probably create your own acronyms and mnemonics when you need to memorize. When giving a speech, assist the audience by (a) recognizing, (b) inventing, and (c) sharing associations. What you have already learned about using comparison to enhance memory is another strategy of association to promote memorization.

6. *Incorporate repetition, audience participation, and practice.* Help your listeners to remember the overall speech and its content by repeating the Thesis and Supporting Claims using the same key phrases every time. It is recommended that you first present this information near the end of the introduction, then within the body between main points, and finally as a summary near the end of the speech. You may also want to repeat other important phrases or statements within the speech for emphasis.

In addition to saying the same words several times, there are other forms of repetition that aid memory such as the repetition of sounds. If you have a series of ideas or objects you want the audience to remember, label each item in the series with a word or phrase that begins with the same letter or sound. A similar ploy is to choose labels that rhyme or have the same internal vowel sounds.

The familiarity that results from repetition allows the audience to play a more active role in the speech. They can anticipate how the speech will develop and begin actively thinking about the content, moving from the role of passive sound receiver to a true communication participant in the speech.

The speaker can also design opportunities for the audience to actively participate in the unfolding of the speech by asking the audience questions, or asking the audience to do something (write, speak, move, imagine) then and there. It is true that "we learn by doing," so find ways for the audience to work with the content of the speech during the time the speech is occurring. Part of the participation may be in the form of practice. You can have the whole group practice by (1) saying something out loud during the speech, (2) saying something silently to themselves, or (3) writing something several times.

■ Key Concepts

Below are some key concepts from this chapter. Test yourself by seeing if you can define and give an example of each of the concepts.

- memory variables

- motivation

- extrinsic rewards

- intrinsic rewards

- high intensity content

- easy memories

- association

- mnemonic devices

- repetition

Chapter Study Guide
You should be able to:
• List the two general categories of memory enhancement that speakers use.
• List and briefly explain the four *Memory Variables.*
• Explain the importance of organization to memory and list three organizational strategies that aid in retention.
• Give guidelines for memory strategies.
• Prepare and present material in speeches using techniques that will help the audience remember the material.

ASSIGNMENT
Memorization (Group Speech)

This oral presentation will be planned and presented as a group activity. Each member of the group should play a role in presenting and each member will turn in the planning sheet. Groups will plan the first day and present the second day.

Length: Between 2 and 4 minutes

Task: Group members will teach the audience new information that the audience will successfully memorize. Presentation must include the following:

1. An explanation of where this content would fit in a complete speech.

2. Why the audience needs to know this information (significance).

3. The use of at least three memorization strategies that teach the information to the audience.

Note Restrictions: Each speaker may use one 4 × 6 notecard if desired. No one is required to use any notes; however speakers are required to hand in either the notecard or a brief outline or map of the part of the speech they presented at the end of the speech. During the oral presentation, speakers should cite any outside materials used.

Preparation: Fill out and turn in the "Speech Planning Sheet." In addition, you should practice and time the presentation as you plan to present it in class.

Memorization Planning Sheet

1. Where will the memorization presentation be used in the complete speech? Include the chosen speech topic and overall Audience Outcome Goal for the speech.

   _____

   _____

2. Which memory enhancing strategies are being used?

   _____

   _____

3. Why should the audience learn this specific information?

   _____

   _____

4. How did you determine that most of the audience members do not already know the information?

   _____

   _____

5. What outside sources did you use as research?

   _____

   _____

6. How long was the presentation in practice? _____ minutes

■ Notecard

Introduction:

Opener:

Where Content fits in complete speech.

Significance for Audience:

Central Claim (and Preview):

Development:

    Memorization Strategy:

    Memorization Strategy:

    Memorization Strategy:

Summary and Conclusion:

Instructor's Evaluation of Memorization

Speaker established an appropriate audience "need to know" _____

Speaker clearly shared Claim (Thesis) _____

Speaker orally shared plan of development _____

Speakers selected effective definitional strategies _____

Speakers maintained audience interest _____

Speakers followed the overall speech plan of introduction, development, conclusion _____

Speech moved toward realization of Audience Outcome Goal (understanding, appreciation, entertainment, persuasion) _____

Individual Speaker Delivery

Speaker maintained a natural, conversational delivery style
Speaker 1   Speaker 2   Speaker 3   Speaker 4

Speaker used voice and body to increase understanding and interest
Speaker 1   Speaker 2   Speaker 3   Speaker 4

Speaker refrained from distracting voice and body behaviors
Speaker 1   Speaker 2   Speaker 3   Speaker 4

Speaker maintained eye contact
Speaker 1   Speaker 2   Speaker 3   Speaker 4

Speaker projected confidence
Speaker 1   Speaker 2   Speaker 3   Speaker 4

Instructor's Evaluation of Memorization

Speaker established an appropriate audience "need to know" _____

Speaker clearly shared Claim (Thesis) _____

Speaker orally shared plan of development _____

Speakers selected effective definitional strategies _____

Speakers maintained audience interest _____

Speakers followed the overall speech plan of introduction, development, conclusion _____

Speech moved toward realization of Audience Outcome Goal (understanding, appreciation, entertainment, persuasion) _____

Individual Speaker Delivery

Speaker maintained a natural, conversational delivery style

Speaker 1   Speaker 2   Speaker 3   Speaker 4

Speaker used voice and body to increase understanding and interest

Speaker 1   Speaker 2   Speaker 3   Speaker 4

Speaker refrained from distracting voice and body behaviors

Speaker 1   Speaker 2   Speaker 3   Speaker 4

Speaker maintained eye contact

Speaker 1   Speaker 2   Speaker 3   Speaker 4

Speaker projected confidence

Speaker 1   Speaker 2   Speaker 3   Speaker 4

ASSIGNMENT
Report on Outside Speech #2: Support Materials

This report will be based on a live speech (not taped, television, or radio) which you will have experienced no more than a week prior to the date the assignment is due. Possible live speeches include (a) classroom lectures (not in this class), (b) sermons or homilies, (c) guest speakers at organizations or public forums, (d) work-related training lectures, or (e) motivational speeches. There are of course other possibilities. You may not use a student speech from a class. The report should be typed and be *no more than three pages* long.

Your report will include the following:

1. Information about the **Speaker**: name, credentials.

2. Information about the **Setting**: location, time of day, size of room, special physical problems in the room (such as temperature, visibility of speaker).

3. Information about the **Audience**: number of people present, reasons why they have chosen to attend, level of enthusiasm for speaker and speech, degree of similarity of audience members (same age? gender? level of education? job or career experiences?)

4. Information about **Global Decisions**.

   Topic: stated topic, narrowed topic

   Speech Goals: primary Audience Outcome Goals stated by speaker or assumed from context, primary Outcome you experienced, secondary Outcomes either stated or experienced, application you will make from cognitive or affective changes.

   Thesis: thesis either stated or extracted from speech by you, presence or absence of narrowed topic and how topic would be developed.

   Main Points: Main Points either stated or extracted from speech by you, wording strategies used to label Main Points, mutually inclusive relationship of Main Points to Thesis.

5. Report and analysis of **Support Materials**: *Narration, Definition, Description, Comparison, Memory Strategies.*

   Report each time the speaker uses one of these support materials. Include the following information about each: (1) type of support material, (2) brief summary of what speaker said, (3) claim supported, (4) your evaluation of effectiveness of the specific support.

6. Conclude your paper with a paragraph evaluating the overall use of support materials by this speaker. You will want to judge which types and which specific examples worked best or failed and why. You may also want to draw conclusions related to frequency of overall concrete support, frequency of specific categories, and variety of categories used.

CHAPTER **10**
Evidence

Chapter Objectives
After reading the chapter you should be able to:
• Distinguish between claims that require evidence for support from those that do not.
• Recognize what evidence makes a claim acceptable.
• Select evidence appropriately in support of a claim.
• Present evidence appropriately for a public speech.

Introduction to Evidence

Our world is faced with a diversity of claims. When we listen to speeches or news reports, read books or magazines, or converse with others, people express their beliefs about objects, people, and events. Many of the claims that people make do not seem unusual at all, some are eccentric, and a few are dangerous. Support for these claims may be based on their experience, education, or indoctrination. Consequently, some are well-justified, while others are stated only because of a person's gut feelings.

Of course, many claims are erroneous either because they are incoherent, inconsistent with other beliefs, or conflict with the facts. Prudence should prevent us from accepting every claim we hear from every person. Our need to resolve tensions between someone else's claims and our own beliefs moves us to assess the truthfulness of their claims or our beliefs. When we listen to others we must sort through their claims and resolve our doubt or disbelief in them as best we can.

Some concept of truth is required in our communication with others, or else there is no way to resolve the claims of others against our own understanding of the world. Occasionally, our own background experiences serve to provide a check against what we hear from others. However, as the claims of people become removed from our own day-to-day experience, the checkpoints become less firmly grounded in experience and, as listeners, we cannot always rely uncritically on what others say. A thoughtful person demands that the claims of others be appropriately justified to gain our belief.

Two and a half thousand years ago, in ancient Greece, the first systematic attempt was made to establish some sort of common ground for belief. By adhering to agreed standards for rational discourse, it was hoped that the disagreements, confusion, and strife, which so often characterize human affairs, could be resolved. The idea was to devise a set of standards for rational discourse that any reasonable person would accept. The standards would then form the basis for settling disputes.

The standards for rational discourse entail providing evidence for claims. This chapter is primarily concerned with the process of devising suitable standards for evidence with which to support claims. Speakers are responsible for providing acceptable support for their claims because an audience is better served when a speaker's support meets specific standards.

Devising Standards for Accepting Claims

What sorts of claims can be reasonably made? One might decide a claim is acceptable insofar as both the speaker and audience simply agree that it is true. For instance, imagine that a representative of the tobacco industry claims to an audience of smokers that smoking has no relationship to cancer. Both the audience and the representative may agree that smoking and cancer are not related. But, you should be uncomfortable with the decision to support a claim on the basis of simple agreement. Simple agreement cannot be acceptable, because there is no standard outside the agreeing parties by which to evaluate the truthfulness of the claim. Moreover, it does not provide any means for resolving disputes between people who disagree at the outset.

A more thoughtful procedure would be to introduce general standards that make some claims more reasonable than others. A speaker then has to find evidence that *appropriately* meets the standards for acceptable support of a claim. An informed audience requires more rigorous forms of evidence for a claim than in informal communication. In courts of law, for instance, hearsay generally does not meet rigorous standards of evidence and cannot be entered into the courtroom as factual testimony.

The standards for acceptable support suggest a functional relationship between the reliability of the claim and the supporting material. In this chapter we describe general standards for making a claim reasonable or acceptable to an audience. The chapter presents four sorts of claims that are reasonably acceptable: (1) *those that are self-evident,* (2) *those based on observation,* (3,) *those based on testimony,* and (4) *those based on circumstance.* Given the standards, speakers must then decide how to best support their claims. Each standard will be discussed and illustrated in the pages following.

Claims Requiring No Support

Surprisingly, one type of claim requires no support at all. Suppose that a speaker were to claim in an argument that "Politicians are human, too." Does the audience have to observe this to know it is true? Aside from all jesting about politicians, you are likely to say that a politician *is* a human. In fact, if someone were to seriously claim otherwise, you would say that the person does not know the meaning of the word politician. There are many claims like the one above. On face value we know that (a) hounds are dogs, (b) bachelors are unmarried, (c) kittens are young, (d) no one can steal his or her own property, and (e) water is wet. **Self-evident claims** are acceptable because of the meaning of the words in the claim, not because of the way things are in the world.

Any speaker can state one of two types of self-evident claims. The first is acceptable because of the *meaning* of the words that make up the claim.

- All rectangles have four sides.

- All women are female.

- You never get a second chance to make a first impression.

- $3 - 2 = 1$

The meaning of the words "rectangle," "woman," "first impression," "minus," and "equals" are what make these claims acceptable. Because a "rectangle" is defined as a "polygon with four sides," you do not have to observe any particular rectangle to know that this claim is true. Similarly, a "woman" is defined as a "'female human being," which makes the claim true.

Another variety of self-evident claims are true because of their form, as in the following:

* An eye is an eye.

* Every dog that is brown is a dog.

* Either it is raining or it is not raining.

* If this is a book, then it is a book.

Each claim above is an instance of a general logical truth: "A is an A," 'Every A that is B is an A," "Either A or not A," "If A, then A." Since the claims are logical truths, you are not required to know anything about eyes, dogs, rain, or books to know that the claims are acceptable. In fact, you could substitute other subjects in each claim and still have a reasonable statement.

In contrast to self-evident claims, there are other claims that depend on something different for their truth. Though it may seem obvious that (a) the planet Saturn has rings, (b) carrots grow underground, or (c) there are more grains of sand on the beach than stars in the sky, these claims depend on the observation of things in this world for their truth. These are called **empirical claims** and they require evidence.

"It's hot," "that's a buffalo." "the rock is green," "natural gas is escaping from the pipe" are all **testable**. That is, you can observe how things are in the world to determine the acceptability of the claim. The difference between *self-evident claims* and *empirical claims* depends on how we come to know their truth.

* Listeners establish the truthfulness of **Empirical Claims** by means of their own observation, or by analyzing circumstances or the testimony.

* **Self-evident Claims** are established by knowing the meaning of words.

Occasionally, self-evident claims make their way into arguments that a speaker is developing. For instance, given the claim about politicians, you might find it in an argument, like the following:

All humans try to protect their egos.
A politician is a human, too.
So, politicians try to protect their egos.

The only claim that requires evidence is the one that states: "All humans try to protect their egos." This claim is not based on the meaning of words, but on how things are in the world. We learn how to provide evidence for this kind of claim below.

Using Direct Observation to Support Claims

In **direct observation**, a speaker appeals to the listener's senses to make a claim acceptable.

* "As you can see in the picture, the building has a complex and elaborate design of intertwined flowers and foliage."

* "Can you smell the gas in this container? It is H_2S."

* "Linen feels different from silk. I'll pass the two around so you can touch them."

* "The sound of a humpback whale is different from a blue whale as you will hear."

As you read over the examples, you might note the similarities between direct observation and the material in Chapter 6 on sensory definitions.

The aphorism, *seeing is believing*, suggests that our own immediate observation of an event can be a direct source of evidence for a claim. Whereas the testimony of speakers, even experts, requires us to make an inference about their authority, direct observation can be quite convincing.

However, direct observation in a public speaking situation is only possible when the speaker shares objects or a demonstration with the audience. Perhaps you have watched as a salesperson demonstrated some product or taken a science class in which the instructor demonstrated some principle of science. A demonstration in a science class is a form of direct observation that is more akin to an experiment. In it, a hypothesis is presented about what is likely to happen, and then the demonstration is performed. The purpose is to determine if the demonstration matches expectations.

We are not saying, however, that direct observation of one's senses always provides infallible information by which to check the acceptability of someone's claims. Many factors can conspire to adversely affect the reliability of observation. Dim light, distance, nearsightedness, and other factors can make vision unreliable. Whispers, mumbling, and loud noises can prevent someone from hearing clearly. A multitude of factors can prevent us from getting reliable information from our senses.

In addition, listeners may not possess the required knowledge to interpret direct observation in a correct or useful way. Many of us, for instance, have had the experience of looking at a plant or animal cell for the first time through a microscope and have not been able to interpret what was seen. Only later, when we learned to differentiate the various parts of a cell could we describe what we were seeing. Sometimes we have to be in a position to know what we are looking at before a correct interpretation can be made.

Another problem with direct observation is that we do not always notice all the details, but may group observations in large categories. We may only notice that a car is "going by quickly" or a house is "large and stately," and fail to notice their color or age. Sometimes the details that are missed are important. A lawyer, for instance, may impeach the credibility of an eyewitness of an event for failing to recall all the details sufficiently.

Despite the problems with direct observation, it still provides a common basis for discerning the truthfulness of a claim. The problems only suggest that direct observation cannot be accepted uncritically. When we are an eyewitness to an event, we should anticipate that others may ask us what we saw, whether we were in a position to see it well, and whether we saw the important details. They are being rational and intelligent when they do so. Although direct observation may assist a speaker in conveying the truthfulness of a claim, there are other means of support.

Using Testimony to Support Claims

In public speaking, testimony is the most common basis for supporting a claim. **Testimony** is a statement of fact or opinion, given by a speaker or someone else, which serves as the basis for belief. For instance, an example presented in a speech—whether it is yours or someone else's, is testimony. Testimony is used in a wide array of intellectual and practical applications. We rely on it for our grasp of history, economics, politics, geography, and science. In addition, which plane to board, what off-ramp to take, where to eat, which building to find a class in, where to find a weather report on TV—all are decided by means of testimony.

Types of Expert Testimony

Three general types of expert testimony can be identified:

(1) expert opinion,

(2) statistics, and

(3) factual data.

The first source of expert testimony is expert opinion. **Expert opinion** often is given on subjects for which there seems to be no right answer—different experts argue differently. Issues associated with morality (i.e., Is abortion right?), religion (i.e., Is there life after death?), and art (Is

Shakespeare the greatest dramatist?) often entail questions that have no definitive answer—only reasoned judgment. That does not mean that in these subjects one person's opinion is as good as another's. Some people have come to their opinion through informed investigation and careful consideration of the subject.

> *Expert Opinion* is **soft evidence** because there is no single right answer. **The experts** have come by their opinion through careful work to reduce the likelihood of ill-informed claims.

Speakers make a mistake when they avoid consulting any experts on such subjects. Presentations that lack expert opinion may include claims that seem ill-informed, naive, or even incorrect. Without deferring entirely to the opinion of soft experts, you should consult them, since they are in a position to have well-developed views. Your presentation will be more convincing when your own judgment has been made against a background of informed judgment.

> *Statistics* and *Factual Data* of expert testimony are **hard evidence**. Claims, about which there is hard evidence, are more certainly true or false. Usually this testimony comes in the form of statistics or factual data.

The second source of expert testimony is statistics. **Statistics** are numbers produced from data that has been organized and analyzed, and the number either summarizes the data or describes relationships among the data. For instance, suppose that the weight for the offensive line (i.e., center, guards, and tackles) of a football team is: 280, 296, 302, 265, 270. Their average or mean weight is 283. Yet, there is no member of the offensive line that weighs exactly 283. The number merely summarizes the mean weight of the line.

Because statistics are derived from data that have been organized and analyzed, it is important to cite the specific source so listeners can evaluate its credibility. The same determination of the source's authority and lack of bias applies here.

In a speech, it is generally a good practice to round statistics off. Most audiences will not remember or are not interested in figures such as 28.43%, which could just as meaningfully be expressed as "slightly over 28%." Of course, if it is critical for an audience to know the exact number, you should provide them with the details.

It is useful to convert statistics to a comparison where possible. Quantitative data are abstract and difficult for an audience to comprehend. A comparison can help to make abstract data more familiar. For instance, a billion dollars can be described to an audience of consumers as being equal to "spending $1 per minute for 2,000 years." The third source of expert testimony is factual data. **Factual data** is produced from measurements (e.g., a yard stick, weight scale, or temperature gauge), direct observation by an expert, or historical record (i.e., the accumulation of early historical texts and archaeological discoveries).

It consists of:

(1) **quantitative data** (i.e., "The salary of the University President is $150,000 per year."),

(2) **informative statements** (i.e., "The even numbered interstate highways run east and west, while the odd ones run north and south."),

(3) **examples** (i.e., "An example of an interstate highway that runs north to south is I-35. It runs from Minnesota to Texas."), and

(4) **exhibits**, like photographs, artifacts, video or tape recordings, etc.

For controversial points, it is important to present multiple independent sources for evidence. Occasionally, a source will not be correct. For instance, sometimes a secondary source will misrepresent an original source. If possible, you should always check the original source. Sometimes factual data is gathered badly by a source and the information in it is simply wrong.

The Acceptable Use of Testimony

Under the appropriate conditions, testimony is an acceptable form of support. An audience will be more inclined to rely on the testimony of others if they are convinced that the *source of evidence* is (1) *in a position to know the facts* and (2) is *unbiased* on the issue. In courts of law the testimony of witnesses is judged on both counts. Attorneys in cross-examination must keep a watchful eye on a witness' testimony, scrutinizing it for vulnerability to truth. A witness may falter in recalling events, use faulty reasoning, or fail to judge properly. In each case the cross-examining attorney must discover if the witness really is in a position to know about the event on which he or she is being cross-examined.

Sometimes, witnesses are in a position to know about an event, but may lie about it. Usually, they favor a particular point of view or outcome in a case, so they are biased. Cross-examining lawyers must also learn to detect possible sources of deviousness, deception, and dishonesty. As a speaker, you should be prepared to describe to the audience just how your sources of evidence are in a position to know and are unbiased.

Being In a Position to Know

Let's say you want directions to a restaurant that recently opened for business in a big city. You would not accept the word of a person who is utterly naive about the location of anything in the city. Similarly, we cannot be expected to accept a claim from someone, unless that person is in a position to know about the claim. Who is in a position to know?

Depending on your speech topic, many types of individuals may be in a position to know. Anyone who is an eyewitness to an event is in a position to know about the event as long as the testimony is restricted to observations, feelings, and memories. Audience members are more likely to rely on the words of speakers when they are describing what they saw, felt, or thought about as the event unfolded. But an audience will not necessarily rely on the words of eyewitnesses for their interpretation and evaluation of an event. Of course, if you rely on an eyewitness, you are assuming that the memory of the eyewitness is accurate. Yet, all things being equal, an eyewitness is probably in a better position to know than someone who has not seen the event.

Often we must accept the word of a person who has not had direct observation of an event. In these cases, audiences are more apt to rely on a source who has a *public reputation for reporting events* accurately, such as major newspapers or TV news services. Collectively, the researchers, reporters, and editors of these publications are in a position to know about the events on which they report. However, some publications such as *The National Enquirer, The Globe,* or *The Weekly World Report* are too unreliable to be sources of accurate information and most audiences will not accept them. Before offering evidence from any publication, we should know its source so we can consider the source's credibility.

Finally, some people are in a position to know because they are **experts**. An expert is someone who has specialized knowledge on a subject based on a combination of education and experience. When people are experts on a subject, they "speak with authority" on that subject. Consequently, they can be cited in a speech as evidence for some claim (see the following Guidelines for Citing a Source).

Speakers can make errors when they provide expert testimony in a speech. One error is misapplying a person's expertise to an inappropriate topic. For instance, a Ph.D. in American history is not necessarily a reliable source on football; a politician is not necessarily a reliable source on health care; and a minister is not necessarily a reliable source on drug addiction.

Another common mistake is for a speaker to make claims like "Scientists generally agree that the universe was created from the "big bang." The use of "scientists" in the sentence is misleading as we have no idea what the speaker means by a "scientist." Do the scientists in the speaker's sentence consist of physicists, biologists, psychologists, or engineers? Moreover, how many scientists are we talking about? Without more information this is an inappropriate use of expert testimony.

Being Unbiased

It is not always enough for a person to be in a position to know. Sometimes, the audience has to know that the person's testimony is unbiased. A person has a **bias** to the extent that he or she has a vested interest in establishing a particular point of view or obtaining a particular outcome. For instance, we would suspect a judge in an international sporting competition who consistently gave his or her country's competitors higher scores than the competitors of other countries. Also, we would suspect a person who is an expert on drug addiction, but is being paid by the tobacco companies to claim that cigarettes are not addictive. In these cases the judge and the spokesperson for the tobacco companies have a *conflict of interest* that may affect their point of view.

A conflict of interest will compromise the objectivity of anyone's judgment. Even an eyewitness or an expert can have their judgment impaired. Consequently, both speakers and listeners should be careful about accepting the point of view of someone who has a conflict of interest. In these cases it is best to look for additional evidence that certifies their testimony.

Using Circumstance to Support a Claim

Jurors listen to two types of evidence in a court of law: testimony and circumstantial evidence. Neither is more important than the other as a means of discerning a claim's truth. **Circumstantial Evidence** consists of accompanying or attendant facts, events, or conditions that point to a claim. The set of circumstances constitutes marks or indications that some particular claim is likely true.

For instance, someone may actually see one car hit another, or someone might infer that one car hit another by observing skid marks, dents in fenders, and the placement of the cars relative to each other. The former is direct observation, while the latter is circumstantial evidence for the collision. Similarly, a person might tell another that he is sorry for his actions, or the offended person might infer remorse as a result of receiving flowers from the offending party). In this case the former is testimony, while the latter is circumstantial evidence for contriteness.

The facts, events, or conditions of circumstantial evidence are factual data (i.e., quantitative data, informative statements, examples, and exhibits), while the claims are **hypotheses**. A hypothesis is guesswork; a conjecture about what happened or will happen given some set of circumstances. It fills gaps in our understanding of something when direct observation, testimony, or self-evident truths do not suffice.

A hypothesis invents a plausible description of what might have happened or what could happen. When we lack direct observation or eyewitness testimony, we frame a plausible scenario to explain piecemeal events. However, the advancement of a hypothesis to explain the events should not be taken lightly. A successful hypothesis for circumstantial evidence depends on three conditions.

- *First, the hypothesis should be phrased affirmatively.* A negatively worded statement, like "Jones did not *steal* from *the* store" does not provide us with much information. It does not serve to explain what happened at the store.

- *Second, the hypothesis must be consistent with the relevant circumstances.* All relevant circumstances must point to the alleged hypothesis, and no relevant circumstance may indicate otherwise. If a hypothesis conflicts with any relevant circumstance, either the "evidence" on the circumstance or the hypothesis is just plain wrong, and only deeper probing will determine which is wrong.

- *Third, the hypothesis should employ no more assumptions than necessary to explain the relevant circumstances.* For instance, if a stranger bumps into you on a crowded sidewalk and apologizes for it, the hypothesis that "this person is awkward" requires fewer assumptions than "this person wants to annoy me." On these grounds, clumsiness is a better hypothesis because it frequently occurs and lacks the assumption of intentionality. More circumstances than presented above are required to assert the hypothesis of annoyance. We need to know, for instance, that the stranger frequently bumps into you but no one else, and/or has a motive.

It is popularly presumed that direct observation is more reliable than circumstantial evidence. Seeing is believing, we are told, and the most reliable kind of evidence is based on direct observation or eyewitness testimony. But, circumstantial evidence can be quite significant and conclusive when it is properly dovetailed. Seeing and hearing are not infallible senses, as we have shown, while a chain of circumstances can be quite convincing. In a court of law eyewitnesses may forget details or lie, but circumstances cannot. Hair, clothes, fingerprints, handwriting, chemical analysis of blood, and other forensic evidence become the clear basis for conviction.

Most scientific theory relies heavily on circumstantial evidence. No one has observed gravity, but such a force is hypothesized because of the attraction of objects to each other (e.g., apples and other things fall to earth when dropped). Circumstantial evidence requires both a set of relevant circumstances and a competent reasoning process. That is, there is a set of circumstances about which we can infer a hypothesis (or claim). In order to develop a strong case, we require many circumstances and all must be consistent with the hypothesis. We now turn to the manner in which evidence is selected so that it can be given proper weight with listeners.

■ Selecting Evidence for a Speech

When audience members listen to a speaker's claim, they assess the claim against their own background experiences. At any point in time, all of us have accumulated a complex set of experiences. We have seen, read, listened, and heard many different things about which we now hold beliefs. We likely believe that (a) all humans have hearts, (b) Japan is economically strong, (c) marathon running requires good health and endurance, and (d) the earth revolves around the sun. In each case our own experiences provide a rational basis for these beliefs. It is likely then that most audience members will not object to a speaker's claim that reflects their background experiences.

However, claims that are not so obvious require support. For instance, if someone told you that he or she knows of a woman who had 45 children over her childbearing years, you would likely not believe it. The claim seems outlandish primarily because it is not in accord with our background experiences. Without proper support, you might think that the person telling you this is joking, mistaken, or trying to deceive you. When listeners reject a suspicious claim, they are not being dogmatic, especially when no convincing evidence is given. We would err seriously if we failed to analyze a speaker's claims with respect to our experiences and the speaker's evidence. Failure to do so will lead us to think that all claims are equally believable.

Audiences will resist some claims without proper support. Many speeches, of course, begin with the speaker and audience sharing certain assumptions that do not require extensive support. In fact, it is prudent to begin a speech on undisputed territory. But, a worthwhile presentation must move to positions that are not initially held by the audience. The **Rule for Supporting Claims** in a speech is a simple one: be capable of supporting any claim an audience member is unwilling to accept. A major function of audience analysis is to discover which claims are likely to meet with resistance.

Tests of Evidence

In selecting evidence for presentation, a speaker should bear in mind that most of us have higher ordered beliefs—beliefs about beliefs—that guide us in assessing the reliability of evidence. Many of us believe that, for instance, information gathered from the *New Encyclopedia Britannica* is more reliable than the *National Enquirer*. We also believe that it is more reliable when we can see something than when we cannot. Further, a new atlas is more reliable than an old one. These higher ordered beliefs are **tests of evidence**.

A speaker helps his or her case measurably when the evidence selected for presentation is tested for reliability. In general, the following probes are tests of evidence and a speaker should keep them in mind as he or she selects evidence for use in a speech.

Tests of Evidence
• Is the evidence obviously relevant to the claim?
• Are conditions favorable to making observations clearly?
• Are the testimony or circumstances accurately represented in the speech?
• Is the source who is cited in the speech unbiased and in a position to know?
• Have you obtained the most recent evidence?
• Are all individual pieces of evidence consistent?

The last test above is a general test for any type of evidence. We often do best when we can assess a body of evidence taken as a whole. Anyone who fixes machinery (e.g., watches, lawn mowers, or computers) does so by observing all the parts working in unison, not by observing each part separately. It is in light of the full body of evidence that we are able to make a more clear assessment of each piece. To see that this is so, review the story of the woman who bore 45 children. Each of you likely rejected or accepted the story based on how well it accorded with your background beliefs. We reject a belief as false if it is inconsistent with other beliefs, and accept it as true if it is consistent with those beliefs.

A speaker will better when he or she can show that the full body of evidence points to the same claim. In fact, this is exactly the practice of attorneys in courts of law. If some testimony or circumstantial evidence is inconsistent with other evidence, then attorneys will probe more deeply to find the weakness. Generally, you probe to reject the least firmly supported evidence. A witness is impeached for unreliability or some circumstantial evidence is on shaky grounds. Consistency among the pieces of relevant evidence is the lighthouse beacon that permits passage through the fog of claims.

The Speaker's Role in Doing Research

A speaker further helps his or her case when the audience perceives that the speaker has done his or her homework. Audience members are more apt to trust the word of a speaker who has gathered a significant body of information on his or her subject than one who has not. While the topic of a speech will partly determine how much detailed knowledge is required to establish your expertise, you can give a credible account of yourself by the way you have prepared information and presented evidence for your speech. In fact, some rapport can be established with the audience if you describe how your own interest in the subject led you to gather information on it. Based on the material for developing introductions (see Chapter 8), a speaker might make the following remarks:

> I took an interest in the subject of multiple sclerosis when my sister was diagnosed with the disease. Once I was aware of some of the research breakthroughs being discovered, I began reading more about it in the media. Now I am aware of how many sources of information are available to the public which I hadn't considered in the past.

You should always do your homework well enough that you are capable of defending your evidence against the sharpest criticism. In cases where it matters, people scrutinize a speaker's evidence for flaws, and "evidence" will be undermined if flaws are found. A proper defense begins with applying the tests of evidence above to your own topic. The following is a discussion of how to present evidence to an audience.

◼ Presenting Evidence in a Speech

Most of the evidence used in a speech will consist of testimony. It is often the case that speakers supply testimonial evidence in a quotation from a source. Though some quotations are mildly interesting, they often are too long and only obliquely refer to the point the speaker wishes to make. In general, keep quotations short. Sometimes, it is better to paraphrase the original source. There is nothing unethical about paraphrasing a source as long as your interpretation maintains the meaning of the source's words.

Citing a Source

When citing a source in a speech, you should do it simply and adhere to the following guidelines.

Guidelines for Citing a Source

- Cite the **name of the person** responsible for the testimony, if known. If the testimony was produced by a staff writer for a newspaper (e.g., *New York Times* or *Washington Post*) or magazine (e.g., *TIME* or *Newsweek*), cite the **periodical**. In addition, if the testimony copies from a book, cite the **title of the book**.

- Always cite the **date of publication** for a printed source or, if you interviewed someone, cite the **date of the interview**.

- **Describe the reputation** of your sources, if they are not well-known to the audience. At least, describe their **field of expertise** or **position** within the business/institution that gives them their credibility. If possible, you should describe their **years of experiences** and/or **their reputation** among peers in their field.

Visual Aids

Occasionally, evidence in a speech will be in the form of a visual aid. A model, diagram, picture, or demonstration often provides the audience with direct observation of some phenomena or circumstantial evidence. A chart or graphic illustration, such as a line or bar graph, pie chart, or comparison graphs can provide a form of testimonial evidence. Thoughtful speakers use visual aids frequently because some material can be presented more quickly and accurately with a visual aid than by words alone. Simple and imaginative visual aids can have a dramatic impact on the audience.

You need not be an artist, buy expensive materials, or toil for hours making an effective visual aid. You need a touch of imagination and a huge sheet of paper for most of them. Some guidelines for presenting visual aids to the audience are presented below.

Guidelines for Presenting Visual Aids

- **Prepare the visual aid in advance of the speech**. If the visual aid consist of a few numbers, they can be written on the chalkboard as you deliver your presentation. But a more complicated illustrations such as a pie chart or bar graph, must be prepared in advance.

- **Make it large enough for everyone to see**. Do not distract the audience's attention by forcing them to strain at small print.

- **Keep it simple and attractive**. A visual aid is an aid, not a complete source of information. You do not need to pack a lot of information into a single visual aid. The simpler the aid, the more likely the audience will be able to focus their attention on you and your presentation.

- **Keep it covered when it is not in use**. When a visual aid is not in use, it is distracting. An audience will attempt to decipher it and will not give you their undivided attention. You are better off not showing it until it is needed.

- **Point to it when you talk**. Occasionally, you need to have the audience focus the attention on some aspect of the visual aid. Consequently, you should learn to point to the relevant parts of the visual aid when you are making some point in your presentation.

- **Avoid focusing your speech toward the aid, rather than your audience**. You can retain the audience's attention longer by maintaining eye contact. If you are thoroughly familiar with the contents of your illustration you need not focus your own attention on it.

ACTIVITY **10.1**
Exercises Testing Chapter Definitions

A. Which claims are **self-evident** and which are **empirical**?

   1. A show is a show.

   2. A triangle has three sides.

   3. Smith drinks too much.

   4. A cabbage is a vegetable.

   5. Most tables are 36 inches in height.

   6. All mushy nauseating things are nauseating.

B. What type of evidence is offered in support of these claims? Is it **direct observation, testimony,** or **circumstance?**

   1. The streets look wet. It must have rained.

   2. This gas canister is nearly empty. You are almost out of gasoline.

   3. Smith, our neighbor, told me that he made a lot of money in the stock market.

   4. Look at Fred across the street. See how he staggers! He's drunk.

   5. Our daughter wrote us from Nepal and told us that they use a calendar that is different from our Western calendar.

   6. If Congress wanted to reform its spending habits, it could. Many intelligent men and women have been elected to Congress and they know how to do it.

C. What evidence would you want to hear *before accepting* these claims? Is it **direct observation, testimony,** or **circumstance**?

   1. People in Wamego go to the movies fewer times than people in Manhattan per year.

   2. The Democrats will hold a majority in both houses of Congress at the end of the next election.

   3. The Japanese celebrate New Year's for a whole week.

   4. There is a higher fat content in the beef at Store A than at Store B.

ACTIVITY **10.2**
Testing Strength of Sources*

Based on the previous criteria given, decide which source in each set constitutes the strongest expert testimony. Provide a reason (i.e., Who is in the best position to know the truth? Who is most unbiased?) for your choice. Second, using the guidelines for citing testimony, cite the source properly as you would in a speech.

SET 1.

A. Matt Brenengen, first-year law student at William Mitchell School of Law, states that unemployment in Minneapolis, MN is at a record low.

B. A 1998 random survey of Minneapolis residents (administered by the Minnesota Labor Department) reported that the city's unemployment rate is at a record low.

C. Press secretary for the Minnesota Governor, Annette Smith, declares that the unemployment rate for Minneapolis is at an all time low.

Letter _____ Reason _____

_____

Citation _____

_____

SET 2.

A. According to Paul Greenberg, National Education Commissioner, in the September 16th, 1992 issue of *Time* magazine, based on a sample of 2,000 students, over three-fourths of college students admit that they have cheated on a major exam.

B. Martha White, twelve-year member of the Stillwater School District PTA, thinks that cheating is the number one problem in U.S. high schools.

C. After observing people cheating in all four of her university classes, Heather Holt, Senior in German Studies at the University of Minnesota, believes cheating is a serious problem.

Letter _____ Reason _____

_____

Citation _____

_____

_____

*This activity was created by Leah White, K-State GTA, 1991–1993.

SET 3.

A. Basketball superstar Michael Jordan claims that *Nike* high-tops provide the best protection from ankle injuries.

B. Erik Gray, spokesperson for *Nike, Inc.* claims that *Nike* high-tops provide the best protection from ankle injuries.

C. Walter Bailey, an orthopedist at the Harvard School of Medicine, claims that *Nike* high-tops provide the best protection from ankle injuries.

Letter _____ Reason _____

_____

Citation _____

_____

■ Key Concepts

Listed below are some key concepts from this chapter. Test yourself by seeing if you can define and give examples of each.

- self-evident claims
- expert opinion
- empirical claims
- statistics
- testable claims
- factual data
- direct observation
- circumstantial evidence
- testimony

- hypothesis
- being in a position to know
- rule for supporting claims
- bias
- tests of evidence
- soft evidence
- citing a source
- hard evidence
- visual aids

Chapter Study Guide

You should be able to:

- List two general bases that people might use for accepting claims as "true."

- Identify and explain the four bases for the acceptance of claims and provide examples of each.

- Define *Self-evident Claims, Empirical Claims, Direct Observations, Testimony Circumstantial Evidence,* and *Hypothesis.*

- Identify three sources of *Expert Testimony.*

- Provide guidelines for using *Statistics* effectively in a speech.

- List and be able to apply the six *Tests of Evidence.*

- Give guidelines *Citing Expert Testimony* in a speech.

- Give guidelines for preparing and using *Visual Aids.*

CHAPTER 11
Forming Arguments

Chapter Objectives
After reading the chapter you should be able to:
•   Identifying an argument and its component parts.
•   Distinguish among different types of premises.
•   Recognize serial and linked arguments.
•   Diagram arguments.

Defining Argument

The word **argument** has at least two distinct meanings as used in everyday language. It is common to use the word to apply to a disagreement or quarrel among people. But in this chapter, argument is not about squabbling with others. Instead, we are more concerned with argument as exemplified in the following expressions: "Sue presented clear and thoughtful reasons for a tax increase." "John failed to support his claim that more time is needed to complete the project." "Anne's point on gun control was convincing." These examples refer to a particular meaning for argument in which reasons are given for some issue.

Arguments—the ones that use reasons—can appear in any context and on any subject. They are widely found in newsprint, weekly magazines, television talk shows, public lectures, private conversation, and any of a host of other communication settings. In addition, arguments can reflect our deepest emotions and values ("No war is just if innocent people suffer") or simple matters of taste ("Fish smells bad. I can't eat it").

Arguments are instruments of rational discourse. Whenever a speaker asks an audience to (a) agree with something, (b) disagree with something, or (c) doubt something, an argument has likely been used in the attempt. In general, any time members of an audience are in the process of deciding an issue or changing their mind, an argument is at the center of the process.

Reasoning, Premises, and Conclusions

A speaker expresses an argument whenever a claim is asserted and other claims are offered as reasons in support of it. An argument then is a set of claims, of which one is supported by the others. For instance, the following is not an argument:

> A chilly wind blew in last night. Clouds rolled in around midnight, followed by thunder and lightening, and then it rained, as I watched from my window. I knew that a long and difficult time lay ahead of me this semester.

Though a claim is made (i.e., "...a long and difficult time lay ahead of me this semester"), none of the other claims are reasons in support of it. Given our definition, it is not an argument. By contrast, the following example contains an argument:

> One summer morning during the regular workweek, I looked out my window to see my neighbor who is normally at work. He was dressed in casual attire and loading the family station wagon with suitcases. I remember when we first moved into the neighborhood he told me that he always took a trip with his family during the summer. So, he is probably on vacation now.

The example above offers a reason in support of a claim (i.e., "he is probably on vacation now") and it fits within our definition of what an argument is. In fact, there are several different sorts of support used in the argument:

CLAIMS	SUPPORT
1. My neighbor is at home during normal work hours.	Direct Observation
2. My neighbor takes a family trip during the summer.	Testimony
3. So, he is probably on vacation now.	Claims 1 and 2

Claims 1 and 2 are supported directly by evidence (see Chapter 10 on evidence). But, Claim 3 is inferred from Claims 1 and 2. It is the result of reasoning. By **reasoning**, we mean the ability to infer the appropriate claim from the reasons given as support.

Much of our knowledge is gained from reasoning; that is, it is not gained so much from direct observation or testimony, but by inferring one thing from another. For instance, you might *observe* that you have a high fever, a sore throat, and a hacking cough. Based on that data, you *infer* that you have an upper respiratory infection. Inferring is the process of going from what you do know (Claims 1 and 2) to what you previously did not know

(Claim 3). Arguments are a means of expanding our knowledge and it is important, needless to say, to understand how to do them correctly.

In an argument a **premise** is a claim that provides a reason for accepting another claim, the conclusion. The **conclusion** is a claim that is implied or follows from the premises. An argument then is a set of claims consisting of a conclusion and one or more premises. When a conclusion is drawn from one or more premises, then an **inference** is made. Using these definitions, the example above can be diagrammed as follows:

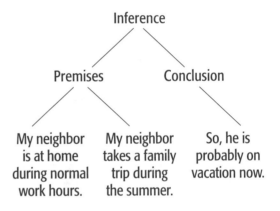

The study of arguments is primarily concerned with inferring or reasoning; in particular, it is focused on what constitutes correct reasoning. Some arguments are good or correct and others are bad or incorrect. The sense in which an argument is good or bad, correct or incorrect, is the subject of the next chapter on evaluating arguments. But, the basis for deciding if an argument is correct hinges on whether the conclusion follows from the premises, or equivalently, whether the premises imply the conclusion.

Recognizing Arguments

In this section we will first discuss the role that language plays in the development of an argument. The language of argument is distinctly different from other ways in which language is used to communicate and these differences are explored. Then, we discuss some useful markers for identifying premises and conclusions. These markers are useful for recognizing and analyzing an argument. Last, we show that the component parts of an argument may not always be explicitly stated. Sometimes, the parts of an argument are omitted in speaking because the listener is likely to know the premises or conclusions anyway.

The Use of Language in Argument

The use of language to form an argument is different from other uses to which language is put. With language, you can promise, thank, curse, congratulate, joke, inspire, and command. But these are distinctly different from the language used to form an argument.

The key to that distinction is the use of language to inform or instruct listeners. One asserts something about the world in order to describe the world and reason about it. In response to assertions made about the world, listeners can ask whether the sentences of an argument are true or false. Compare this with other language uses, such as questions or commands. A question, such as "What should we do about crime?" cannot be evaluated as true or false. A command, such as "Don't be a quitter!" is neither true nor false. It is advice and we can only be concerned with whether it should have been said or obeyed.

Expressive uses of language should also be distinguished from argument. The following few lines from Robert Frost's famous poem, "Stopping by Woods on a Snowy Evening," could not be evaluated as true or false.

> "The woods are lovely, dark, and deep,
> But I have promises to keep,
> And miles to go before I sleep…"

Frost is selecting observations about the world in order to express feeling. A politician may also try to invoke feeling from the audience by quoting expressive lines, such as "God bless America,

land that I love," but these do not make up an argument. To be recognized as an argument, the sentences must be meant to inform us about objects and events in the world and be evaluated as true or false.

Argument Markers

Arguments do not come to us with signs saying "premise" or "conclusion." Occasionally, however, verbal clues may indicate one or the other. **Premise Indicators** include such words and phrases as those shown below.

Premise Indicators

- After all
- And
- As a matter of fact
- Because
- By contrast
- Even so
- For
- Furthermore
- However
- Indeed
- In addition
- In fact
- In support of
- It has been observed that
- Moreover
- Nevertheless
- Of course
- On the one hand…on the other hand
- Seeing that
- Since
- Finally
- Now

"*Because* I think, I am" shows the use of "because" before the premise "I think." Conclusion metaphors include such words and phrases as the following:

Conclusion Indicators

- As a result
- Consequently
- Hence
- It follows that
- So
- The point is
- Therefore
- This implies (or, entails) that
- Thus
- We may conclude that

Much of the time, however, you will not be able to detect which part of the argument is premise and which is conclusion by means of these indicators. You will have to actively think about what in the argument is used as support and what is being inferred. There are even occasions in which you will not be able to detect the premise from the conclusion at all! Examine the following pair of claims:

> This month is May.
>
> Last month was April.

It is equally reasonable to say that the first sentence is a premise and the second a conclusion, as it does to say that the second sentence is a premise and the first a conclusion. It also makes sense to say that these sentences are just unrelated observations and no argument is formed at all. Clearly, you need more context to evaluate whether an argument is being stated and if it is, what is being inferred.

Omitted Parts

Arguments can often have premises or conclusions that are not explicitly stated. Speakers may omit a premise or conclusion because they anticipate that most, if not everyone, can be reasonably expected to fill in the missing parts. Advertisers, for instance, will leave out a conclusion not only because you, the consumer, can be expected to infer it, but also because omission has a persuasive effect. When aspirin was the only over-the-counter pain reliever, a well-known brand of aspirin advertised its product using the following premise:

> Government tests show that no other pain reliever is stronger or more effective than Brand X.

It was anticipated that you would infer the following:

> Brand X is the strongest and most effective pain reliever of all tested brands.

Getting you to infer the "right" conclusion, as if it were your own idea, is simply a means of drawing you into the influence process. Incidentally, the above conclusion is an appropriate inference from the stated premises, but it is not the only inference that might have been drawn. If you think about it, the following conclusion could have been inferred as well:

> Brand X is not any weaker or less effective than any other tested brand.

As it turned out, this last conclusion was the more appropriate one to infer as government tests showed that all brands of aspirin were essentially alike!

Premises can be left out, too. If someone said, "She is so smart! She flies a plane," there is an obvious unstated premise: "Anyone who flies a plane is smart." Conclusions or premises can be omitted in an argument and you, the listener, are expected to produce them. Whether you are developing an argument for a speech or listening to an argument in a speech, you will be required to sort out each element of the argument.

ACTIVITY **11.1**
Identifying Arguments, Premises, and Conclusions

A. Determine whether each passage contains an argument or not. If the passage contains an argument, underline the premises once and the conclusion twice.

1. It is pouring down rain, making the road conditions dangerous for driving. But I must go to the grocery store, even though no one is hungry.

2. You shouldn't kill lady bugs. They eat other insects and pose no threat to humans.

3. Tom was the fastest typist with the fewest number of errors of the people who interviewed for the job. Generally, Mary hires the person who scores the best on the typing test. Tom will likely get the job.

4. Zippy toothpaste has fluoride to prevent tooth decay and a whitening agent to keep teeth looking clean. It is on sale at your local drug store.

5. All shelties will bark at anyone who intrudes on their territory. So, Bonnie will make a good watchdog at her home.

B. Each passage contains a set of premises that can plausibly be understood as having an unstated conclusion. Supply the unstated conclusion.

1. You are driving on an interstate highway through a heavy rainstorm. You notice that only about half of the cars coming in the opposite direction have their windshield wipers on.

Conclusion: _____

2. You went to the post office this morning and saw that the flag was flying at half-mast. Later, you went by the county courthouse and also saw that the flag was at half-mast.

Conclusion: _____

3. After class you go to see your professor about an error he apparently made in adding up your score. You explain that 75 minus 12 is 63, not 53. He tells you that he is too busy to deal with it.

Conclusion: _____

4. Your child, age five, who usually has a good appetite, says no this morning when you offer her a bowl of cereal.

Conclusion: _____

5. Your mother who is normally talkative is silent this morning. When you talk to her, she offers little in return.

Conclusion: _____

Elements of Arguments

The process of developing an inference is one in which several different sorts of premises work together to support a conclusion. According to Stephen Toulmin's now classic essay, *The Uses of Argument*, an argument consists of a set of interlinked premises that support some conclusion.* Some premises provide us with facts, while other premises link the facts to a conclusion. These premises are called **Data** and **Warrant** respectively, and they are defined as follows:

- **Data** are informative claims that provide the basis for the conclusion. They may be based on observation, oral testimony, historical record, accumulated experience, common knowledge, legal precedence, self-evident claims, and the like.

- A **warrant** is a claim that explains the connection of the data to conclusion. Drawing an inference from data to conclusion often requires a more general assumption that links data and conclusion. It is the reason that a conclusion can be drawn from the data.

For the sake of closure, we will reintroduce the conclusion of an argument. A **conclusion** is a claim that follows from data and warrant in the argument. A conclusion is something that the speaker wants to arrive at, and the data and warrant are used to infer the conclusion.

You should notice that each element is defined by its relationship to other elements. With all three elements in place, we are capable of understanding how a speaker is making a point. We may not necessarily agree with the speaker, but we at least know the "course" of the argument. For instance, suppose you are watching a trial on TV in which the defense attorney is giving her summation before a jury when you hear her say,

My client was having lunch with a friend at the Purple Onion in Wichita when the crime in Kansas City occurred. Since he could not have been at two different places at the same time, he did not commit the robbery.

Clearly, the defense attorney is attempting to establish the conclusion that her client is innocent. The first sentence is data. It is an informative sentence that locates the whereabouts of her client at the time of the crime. The last sentence can be broken down into two sentences: one is the position to which the defense attorney wants the jury to agree (i.e., the conclusion) and the other links the data to the conclusion (i.e., the warrant). The complete argument is in the following diagram.

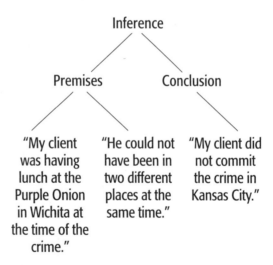

Finally, there is one more element that modifies the conclusion. In some arguments, the premises provide an absolute guarantee of the conclusion. But in other arguments, the premises provide only limited support for the conclusion. The qualifier distinguishes these types of argument as it indicates the strength of relationship between the premises and the conclusion. Its role in analyzing argument will become more important in the next chapter.

A **qualifier** indicates the degree of support for the conclusion. The qualifier is typically embedded in the conclusion itself and consists of adverbs or brief adverbial phrases as:

Qualifier Indicators

- certainly
- probably
- presumably
- likely
- possibly
- plausibly
- maybe
- so apparently
- so far as the evidence goes
- for all we can tell

The following argument requires a qualifier to modify the force of the conclusion. The conclusion is "Lung cancer is probably caused by auto emission wastes" and is diagrammed below.

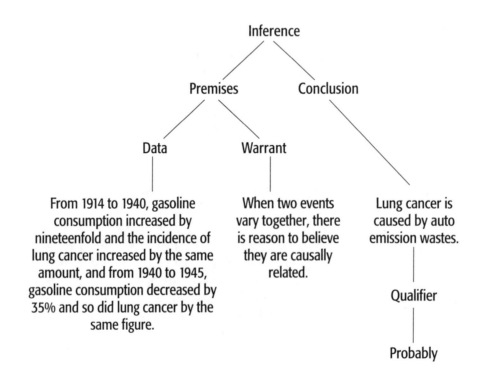

ACTIVITY **11.2**
Diagramming Arguments

Analyze the following arguments and diagram the argument structure by showing the data, warrant, conclusion, and qualifier.

1. A cold front passed through Midwest today as the winds shifted to the northwest, the rain is stopped, and there are breaks in the clouds. When a cold front passes through the region, it is followed by clearing and colder weather. Tomorrow it will be clear and colder than today.

2. Chuck certainly does not treat his wife fairly. He goes out with his buddies many nights of the week, leaving his wife home alone. A husband should not leave his wife at home alone, while he goes out to have a good time.

3. Last year, State U. generated more offense than any other team in the conference and gave up the fewest number of yards on defense. Since most of their players will return this year, it is likely they will be the conference champions.

4. The patient presumably needs penicillin. He has an infection in his wound. The standard practice in these cases is to give the patient penicillin.

5. Mary regularly attends her classes, reads all of her assignments, and studies thoroughly for her tests. Most students who work hard for their classes make passing grades. Mary will likely pass her classes.

■ More Complicated Arguments

Arguments can be of any length. The examples used so far in this chapter have been short because we have viewed an argument as an independent unit. As an independent unit, an argument consists of a set of interlinked claims that support a conclusion. But an argument can also depend on other arguments. That is, smaller arguments can be components of a larger argument. As a result, there is no reason that an argument could not run the length of a book! An elaborate argument, for instance, that democracy is the most viable political system for humans, may require a lengthy system of inter-related arguments that are chained or clustered together to support the main argument.

A **Serial** argument is one in which the conclusion for one argument becomes a premise for another. A chain of these arguments are used to support some final conclusions. The process can be diagramed as follows:

Based on data M
With warrant N
Therefore, conclusion O.

↓

Based on data O
With warrant P
Therefore, conclusion Q.

↓

Based on data Q
With warrant R
Therefore, conclusion S.

Consider the following example of a serial argument:

George was a philosophy major.
Every philosophy major has read Marx.
George has read Marx.

↓

George has read Marx.
Marx demonstrates that capitalism is bound to fail.
George knows that capitalism will fail.

↓

George knows that capitalism will fail.
Anyone who knows that capitalism will fail would not open a hardware store.
George is not opening a hardware store.

Arguments can also be **Linked** together. A linked argument uses several reasons to support the same main conclusion. This can be diagrammed as follows:

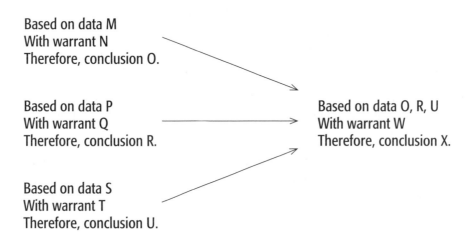

Consider the following example of a linked argument:

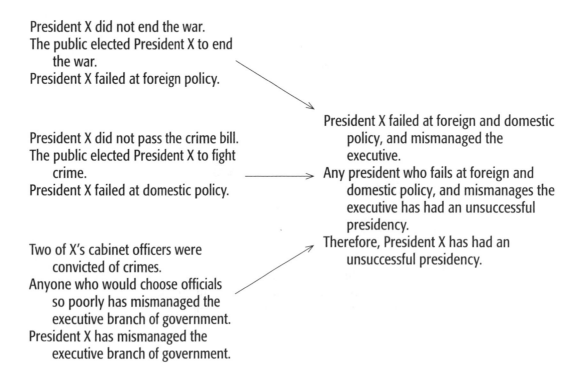

ACTIVITY **11.3**
Identifying and Diagramming Complex Arguments

Each passage contains a complex argument. Pick out each argument, identify its premises and conclusion, determine whether it is a serial or, inked argument, and diagram it completely. Some parts of the argument have been omitted. Simply, write the word OMITTED where a part has been left out.

1. Geothermal energy can supply a plentiful source of energy to consumers that is easier and safer than other conventional energy sources. It has widespread use in the state of California and the country of Iceland, where in both cases, the quantity of energy produced exceeds the demand for energy. So, geothermal energy can provide a plentiful source of energy to consumers. All that is required is to use conventional oil-drilling technology to bore relatively shallow holes a few miles into the earth, pump water down, and use the steam that comes up to drive electric turbines. Other sources of conventional energy require expensive use of more sophisticated technology. So, geothermal technology is easier than other conventional sources of energy. There are no harmful by-products, and there is almost no damage to the environment. All other energy sources produce either more noise, air, or water pollution than geothermal energy. So, it is safer than other sources of energy.

   Argument is serial _____ or linked _____.

2. Various economic indicators reliably show that the cost of living is increasing. When the cost of living increases, past experience has led us to expect that workers will demand increased wages. So, workers will likely demand higher wages. If workers demand higher wages, then we can expect that management will resist the demands of the workers. Thus, labor-management strife is likely. We can expect labor-management strife. In the past, widespread labor-management strife has caused workers to strike. So, we can expect to see a round of strikes in the future.

    Argument is serial _____ or linked _____ .

Strategies for Analyzing Naturally Occurring Arguments

No mechanical procedure exists for sorting the parts of an argument correctly into its elemental categories (i.e., data, warrant, conclusion, qualifier). However, some useful advice can be given that will increase the likelihood of a correct analysis. This advice is provided in three parts below.

1. Identify the basic pattern of reasoning used in the argument.

    a. **Look for premise and conclusion indicators**. These words and phrases, cited earlier, are often the most useful clues to understanding an argument. As you listen to an argument, you should try to pick them out or, if you are reading one, underline them.

    b. **Examine the context of the argument.** Often, the context in which an argument occurs provides information about the intentions of the speaker. The context can serve as a frame of reference that permits us to interpret the various claims developed in the argument. For instance, if someone were to say: "I need to know today's date. It is, I think, the eighth. Yesterday was the seventh." We know from the context that the argument's conclusion is "It is the eighth," while "Yesterday was the seventh" is obviously a premise.

    c. **Identify the components of the like argument**. Arguments have a starting point, an ending point, and several steps in between. An efficient way to sort out the components is to look for the conclusion first and then for the data. Ask yourself what is being resolved or established in the argument. Then, look for the data to support it. Since an argument consists of a set of interrelated claims, you often have to develop a hypothesis about what the conclusion is, then proceed backwards to the data that supports the conclusion, then forwards to find the intermediary steps. This process may occur several times to establish the conclusion.

2. Sharpen the focus of each claim in the argument.

    a. **Rephrase premises and conclusions to clarify them**. Some claims in an argument require clarification. If a question or command appears in an argument, it must be restated as a declarative sentence (see previous discussion on "Argument Language" in this chapter). Other claims appear equivocal and should be restated as assertions. For instance: "I think that Professor Smith is out of her office. I believe she is in class. She can't see you, now." This is not merely a report about what someone thinks, but an argument that should be stated as follows:

    > Professor Smith is out of her office. She is in class. So, she can't see you, now.

    Language is a complex and sometimes complicated system for expressing ideas. When we analyze an argument, we need to be aware of the complexities to understand the premises and conclusions correctly.

    b. **Remove information not essential to the argument**. Everyday arguments are often filled with commentary that are neither premises nor conclusions. To analyze the argument clearly, you will want to remove this material. For instance:

    > You are not paying attention to me when I talk. I am saying that Americans cannot pay for unlimited health care costs. No matter how much moralizing we do, health care will have to be rationed.

If we discard the unnecessary baggage from the argument, we have:

Americans cannot pay for unlimited health care. It will have to be rationed.

3. Identify the main argument and sub-arguments.

a. **Locate the main argument**. All arguments have exactly one central conclusion. This conclusion and its premises are the main argument. Since the central conclusion is the whole point of the speech, you will have to identify it.

b. **Locate sub-arguments**. The premises of the main argument can be supported by subarguments which, in turn, can be supported by more subarguments. Subarguments can form a chain or cluster, or both (see the section on "More Complex Arguments" above). In addition, sub-arguments can assert the reliability of the warrant. Warrants sometimes cannot be accepted on face value and a sub-argument must be formed to back it up. For instance, let's say you are arguing that Sally may be expected to do well at college because she is an honors graduate of North High School and honors graduates of North do well in college. You will want to back up the warrant in the argument by providing evidence, perhaps statistical evidence, that past honors graduates of North have done well.

c. **Locate any rebuttals**. A subargument can also form around the main conclusion that counters any objections that someone might have to the main conclusion. As a speaker, you might anticipate possible objections to your conclusion and argue that the objections are either false or sufficiently rare (i.e., atypical or exceptional) so that the main conclusion is still strongly supported by the premises.

ACTIVITY **11.4**
Diagramming a Naturally Occurring Argument

The following passage contains a complex argument. Pick out each argument, identify its premises and conclusion, determine whether it is a serial or linked argument, and diagram it completely.

> The Palestinian people themselves have varying views as to how the conflict with Israel should be settled. Roughly 60 percent of the world's 3.5 million Palestinians live in Jordan and the Israeli-occupied West Bank and Gaza Strip, and because they face the reality of Israel they are more apt to seek a negotiated compromise. Others, particularly those living in teeming refugee camps in Lebanon and Syria, still harbor desperate dreams of returning to the homes in what was once Palestine but is now Israel. (Angus Deming, "The PLO: A New Image?" *Newsweek*: 3 September 1979, p.24–25).

■ Key Concepts

Listed below are some key concepts from this chapter. Test yourself by seeing if you can define and give examples of each.

- argument
- premise
- conclusion
- inference
- premise indicators
- conclusion indicators

- data
- warrant
- qualifier
- serial argument
- linked argument

Chapter Study Guide
You should be able to:
• Define and explain the relationships among the following concepts: *Argument, Premise, Conclusion,* and *Inference.*
• Identify *Arguments, Premises,* and *Conclusions.*
• Identify *Argument Markers.*
• Define and explain the relationship of the following concepts *Data, Warrant, Conclusion,* and *Qualifier.*
• Diagram arguments.
• Define and identify *Serial* and *Linked Arguments.*
• Provide guidelines for analyzing Naturally Occurring Arguments.

CHAPTER **12**
Analyzing Arguments

Chapter Objectives
After reading the chapter you should be able to:
• Distinguish between deductive and inductive reasoning.
• Define a valid argument.
• Distinguish between validity and soundness.
• Identify and distinguish between four types of inductive arguments: causation, sign, inductive generalization, and analogy.
• Prepare an argument speech using an appropriate topic, AOG, thesis, and properly developed strong arguments that provide reasons to accept the major argument.

Introduction

Both scientists and philosophers alike have claimed that humans are rational animals. We are **rational** not merely because we have the capacity for reason, but because we often look for reasons when something cannot be explained. If we are faced with some significant event, we want a reason that explains why it happened. For example, when an airplane crashes, investigators are dispatched to the crash site to determine whether the crash was due to human error, mechanical failure, sabotage, or an act of nature. No event, we believe, could happen without some reason for it. Our impetus to find an explanation stems from our desire to understand the world in which we live.

A major function of public speaking is to provide cogent or satisfactory reasons for something. Speeches that explain a process, champion a particular point of view, analyze a problem, or pursue a solution to a problem often use reasoning to achieve their objectives. Significantly, many thoughtful individuals believe that speakers *ought* to provide reasons to their audience in order to encourage rational, rather than emotional, responses to issues related to the public good. Aldous Huxley wrote, "Democratic institutions can be made to work only if all concerned do their best to impart knowledge and to encourage rationality." If you subscribe to Huxley's belief in democratic institutions, then you accept the premises that people are capable of reason and require reasons for believing the contents of a public speech.

While it is certainly true that public speeches utilize appeals to vanity, fear, sex, pride, and assorted prejudices, not all audiences will accept the content of these messages. Abraham Lincoln said it best: "you can fool some of the people all of the time and all of the people some of the time, but you can't fool all of the people all of the time." At some point, many people recognize that if they fail to think rationally, then they risk acceptance of falsehoods, endorsement of inferior items, or the failure to achieve the appropriate ends. It is simply in the long-term best interest to be reasonable, so speakers who fail to provide reasons do their audience a great injustice.

Providing good reasons in communication is clearly important and this chapter will consider what that means. In Chapter 11 we defined an argument, described how to recognize one, studied its component parts, and showed how they can be linked together. In this chapter we will be concerned with two types of argument. This is important because both reflect different reasoning and require different criteria for their evaluation.

Types of Argument

The merits of any argument depend on two independent issues: (1) the truth or falsity of its premises and (2) the extent to which its premises support the conclusion. The first issue is a matter of whether individual claims are, in fact, true or false. In the chapter on evidence, we stated that a claim is true when it is either self-evident or appropriately related to reality. The second issue, which is discussed in this chapter, has more to do with **reasoning**, as it focuses exclusively on the relationship of the premises to the conclusion.

Two types of reasoning serve us well: **deductive** and **inductive**. The critical difference between good deductive reasoning and good inductive reasoning lies in the connection between the premises and the conclusion. The following argument is an example of good **deductive** reasoning. As you read the argument, pick out the premises and conclusion. Notice the markers that are used to indicate the premises and conclusion.

Example of Deductive Reasoning

Justice demands restitution for false convictions. But there is no restitution in a capital crime for a false conviction, once the death sentence has been carried out. So, capital punishment has no place in a system of justice.

Given the premises, does the conclusion follow necessarily from them? Now, the following argument is an example of good **inductive** reasoning. Again, pick out the premises and conclusion.

Example of Inductive Reasoning

Persons commit capital crimes from every economic station in life. But a disproportionate number of offenders' sentence with capital punishment are poor. So, capital punishment is employed selectively.

Given the premises, does the conclusion follow necessarily from the premises? If you answered "yes" to the first question and "no" to the second, you may have detected an important difference between the two arguments. Despite their similar subject matter, they differ in the extent to which their premises support their respective conclusions. The conclusion of the first argument *follows with certainty* from its premises. There is simply no doubt that capital punishment is an unjust form of punishment based on the premises of the argument. However, the premises of the second argument provide only *probable support* for the conclusion. There is a strong chance that capital punishment is used selectively, but there is a possibility, no matter how remote, that it is not always used selectively. In brief, this is the difference between deductive and inductive reasoning.

Deductive Arguments

Deductive arguments are meant to be valid; that is, the premises are supposed to lead with certainty to the conclusion. *Only **Deductive Arguments** employ a form of reasoning that strictly follows the rules of logic and, as a result, the premises prove* *the conclusion.* All other arguments have premises that fall short of proving the conclusion beyond any possible doubt.

Deductive arguments are characterized as valid or invalid. The word "valid" when applied to deductive arguments has a special meaning. It does *not* refer to a single sentence or claim; one cannot say that a premise or conclusion by itself is valid because it is true. Deductive validity refers only to the extent to which the premises support the conclusion. An argument is **valid** when it is not possible that the premises are true and the conclusion is false. Any relationship less strong is **invalid**.

Let's take an example to see how this definition is applied to an argument. Is the following argument valid?

> Cars go down 12th Street very fast.
> Any dog hit by a car on 12th Street will be killed.

Most of us are inclined to say the argument is invalid. We know that it is possible, no matter how unlikely, that some dog might survive being hit by a car on 12th Street. The premises do not preclude such a possibility. So, it is possible for the premises to be true and the conclusion false. Since the truth of the premises do not guarantee the truth of the conclusion, the argument is invalid.

A simple thought experiment using Venn diagrams can assist us in analyzing an argument for true premises and a false conclusion. If we find such a possibility, the argument is invalid.

Many claims in an argument involve relationships between collections of ideas which use the words all, some, or no as in (a) "All Kansas rocks are limestone," (b) "Some Kansas rocks are limestone," and (c) "No Kansas rocks are limestone." Each of these claims state a relationship between two sets of objects: the set of Kansas rocks and the set of things that are limestone. But, different relationships are developed depending on the use of all, some, and no.

First, consider the statement "All Kansas rocks are limestone." It means that there are no Kansas rocks that are not limestone. As such, the diagram below depicts the relationship between the two sets. The set of Kansas rocks is a subset of the set of things that are limestone.

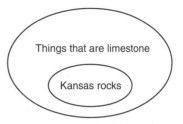

The diagram above contains all of the elements under discussion in the argument.

Next consider the statement "Some Kansas rocks are limestone." It means that there is at least one rock *(or possibly "all")* that is limestone. The Venn diagram below illustrates the relationship described in the statement.

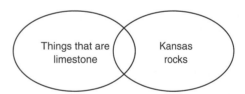

Finally, consider the statement "No Kansas rocks are limestone." This is equivalent to saying that no Kansas rock is a member of the set of things that are limestone, and can be illustrated using non-overlapping (or disjoint) sets as follows.

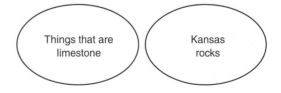

We can now use our knowledge of Venn diagrams to analyze the validity of arguments. In order to prove an argument invalid by means of a Venn diagram, we assume that the premises of the argument are true and look for a circumstance in which the conclusion could be false. The following argument is valid.

> All humans have lungs.
> Sally is a human.
> So, Sally has lungs.

Suppose it is true that all humans have lungs. This is equivalent to saying that the set of humans is entirely contained within the set of things having lungs (see below). Now, suppose that it is true that Sally is a human. Since Sally belongs to the set of humans (as represented by the X below), it follows necessarily that she has lungs, and the argument is valid.

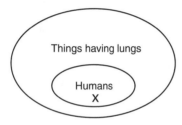

The argument below is also valid.

> No dogs are reptiles.
> Bonnie is a dog.
> So, Bonnie is not a reptile.

Suppose that no dogs are reptiles; that is, the set of dogs do not overlap with the set of reptiles. Non-overlapping sets (or disjoint sets) have no common elements. Suppose, too, that Bonnie is a dog, so Bonnie is contained within the set of dogs (see the X below). It follows necessarily that Bonnie is not a reptile, and the argument is valid.

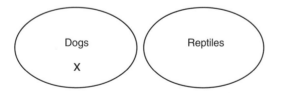

Finally, this argument is valid as well.

> All speeders break the law.
> Bill does not break the law.
> Bill is not a speeder.

Suppose that all speeders break the law. This relationship can be illustrated by making the set of speeders a subset of the set of things that break the law (see below). In addition, suppose that Bill does not break the law. This premise says that Bill is not contained within the set of things that break the law. So, if he is not in that set, it follows necessarily that he cannot be in the set of speeders as well.

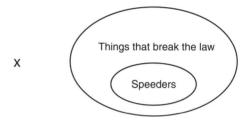

By contrast, consider the following invalid argument.

> Some smokers get cancer.
> John smokes.
> So, John will get cancer.

Suppose that some smokers get cancer. This relationship can be depicted by the two overlapping Venn diagrams shown on the next page. Now, suppose that John smokes. But, where does John go? Should he be placed in the subset of smokers who get cancer or those who don't? The premises do not give us a clue! Since John could be in the set of smokers who don't get cancer, there is one possible circumstance under which the premises are true and the conclusion is false. So, the truth of the premises does not guarantee the truth of the conclusion, and the argument is invalid.

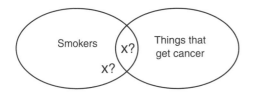

Let's consider another invalid argument.

> Everyone who watches daytime TV gets
>   bored.
> Jane is bored.
> So, there is no denying that Jane has watched
>   daytime TV.

Suppose that everyone who watches daytime TV does get bored. This relationship, of course, can be demonstrated by making the set of daytime TV watchers a subset of things that are bored. In addition, suppose that Jane is bored. Now, we know that Jane belongs in the set of things that are bored, but does she belong in the set of daytime TV watchers? The premises don't say. So, it is possible that she hasn't watched daytime TV, yet she is bored. Under this circumstance, the premises are true and the conclusion false, and the argument is invalid.

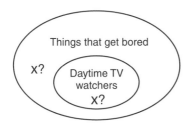

The last argument is also invalid.

> All judges are honest.
> Fred is not a judge.
> So, Fred is not honest.

Suppose that all judges are honest. This, of course, is shown by making the set of judges a subset of the things that are honest. Now, suppose that Fred is not a judge. Given this premise, we know that Fred does not belong in the set of judges, but does he fall necessarily outside the set of things that

are honest? The premises don't say. The premises do not exclude the possibility that Fred is honest. Under this circumstance, the premises are true and the conclusion is false, and so the argument is invalid.

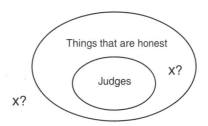

An argument is valid when it is *not possible* for the premises to be true and the conclusion false. The use of Venn diagrams enable you to think of possible ways in which the premises *could* be true and the conclusion *could* be false. If you discover such an instance, the argument is invalid.

Validity, Truth, and Soundness

To this point we have learned that a deductive argument is valid when the conclusion follows necessarily from the premises; that is, *if the premises are true, then the conclusion cannot be false*. At this point it is very easy to become confused since most of us automatically react to invalid arguments as "bad" and a valid argument as "good." But, the situation is more complex than this. Keep in mind that validity does *not* require that the premises be actually true. The sample arguments above only asked you to assume that the premises were true. For instance, the following argument is valid, but has false premises.

> All houses are white.
> All white objects are made of concrete.
> So, all houses are made of concrete.

What makes the argument valid is that if the premises were true—even though they are not —the conclusion would have to be true. Remember that deduction is, first and foremost, concerned with implications of premises, not with sorting out evidence to determine if a premise is true or not. The job of most disciplines, like engineering, physics, psychology, agriculture, and communication, is to determine whether a premise is true or not, but the job of logic is to determine the implications of those premises.

Now, when an argument has a false starting point, it is essentially worthless. It will only be by sheer luck that a true conclusion will follow from a false premise and we will not want to rely on arguments that begin with a false premise. Thus, we will need to make a distinction between the actual truth or falseness of the premises in an argument and the validity of the entire argument.

A **sound** argument is one that has (1) actually true premises and (2) a conclusion that follows necessarily from the premises (i.e., is valid). Soundness is reserved *only* for deductively valid arguments having actually true premises. So, if we begin with actually true premises and apply the deductive rules of inference, as given above, to those premises, we can be sure of inferring actually true conclusions. As a speaker, you must provide evidence for your premises to support their truth. Once the truth of the premises has been established, then deductive rules of inference can be applied to those premises. Any conclusion derived using the rules of inference will certainly be, in fact, true.

ACTIVITY **12.1**
Identify the Valid Arguments

Analyze each of the arguments for validity using Venn diagrams as previously shown. If the argument is valid, state why it is valid. Then, state whether the argument is sound and give a reason.

1. All rich people are well dressed.
    The fellow I met last night was certainly well dressed.
    So, he must be rich.

    Valid or Invalid: _____
    Why? (Show Venn diagram)

    Sound or Unsound: _____
    Why?

2. All people who are deeply moved by the victims of famine in Africa will contribute to the effort
       to alleviate the suffering.
    Sally has been deeply moved by this tragedy.
    So, Sally will contribute to the cause.

    Valid or Invalid: _____
    Why? (Show Venn diagram)

    Sound or Unsound: _____
    Why?

3. Oak trees grow only in places where it rains with some degree of regularity.
   It does not rain in the Sahara with any degree of regularity,
   Oak trees do not grow in the Sahara.

   Valid or Invalid: _____
   Why? (Show Venn diagram)

   Sound or Unsound: _____
   Why?

4. No amount of money will guarantee self-fulfillment.
   Happiness requires self-fulfillment.
   Money cannot guarantee happiness.

   Valid or Invalid: _____
   Why? (Show Venn diagram)

   Sound or Unsound: _____
   Why?

5. Running every day will make you fit.
   Joe does not run every day.
   So, he is not fit.

   Valid or Invalid: _____
   Why? (Show Venn diagram)

   Sound or Unsound: _____
   Why?

Inductive Arguments

A valid deductive argument has premises that guarantee the conclusion, but an inductive argument has premises that provide only probable support for the conclusion. *In **Inductive Reasoning**, we sort out evidence from past experience to reason about some new situation.* Patterns or regularities are noted in our experience and those patterns are projected onto some new situation. For example, the prediction that the sun will rise tomorrow uses inductive reasoning based on the premise that the sun has risen every day in our past experience. If I let go of a stone from some altitude, I expect it to fall because of my experiences with gravity. Notice that I am using my past experience as a guide to a new situation. I don't know that the stone will fall; I just make an educated guess.

The examples above reflect the nuts and bolts of inductive reasoning. There are no guarantees that the conclusion will be true even if the premises are actually true. Since inductive reasoning asserts something about past experience, there is no guarantee that past experience will hold when projected onto a new situation. The conclusion for an inductive argument can only be *probably* true.

In a good inductive argument with true premises, the conclusion will be false some of the time. The premises provide only some degree of support for the conclusion. As evidence mounts, the probability increases, but it is still not certain. So, there is a gap between the premises and the conclusion, and the qualifier "probably" or some such word is often added to the conclusion (see Chapter 11 on qualifiers).

Because the conclusion will be false some of the time with true premises, a good inductive argument is never valid.

Consider this example.

> 98% of the patients recover when injected with penicillin.
> George was injected with penicillin.
> George will recover.

Chances are that George will recover, but it is only probably or likely true. The warrant provides a strong chance for recovery as 98% of the patients have previously done so. But there is some risk that, although the premises are true, the conclusion could be false. We cannot be absolutely sure that the conclusion will be true even though the premises are true.

In contrast to the argument above, consider the following inductive argument.

> 60% of the patients recover when injected with penicillin.
> George was injected with penicillin.
> George will recover.

You will notice that the evidence for George's recovery is not nearly so convincing as in the last argument. It is more likely that George will recover than not, but the conclusion is now more tenuous. It would be even more tenuous if the figures were only 30% or 20%, or even less. At 0%, there is no support for the conclusion that George will recover.

The support for any conclusion in inductive reasoning is always a matter of degree. The argument's success depends on the weight of evidence that can be gathered in support of a conclusion. In a strong inductive argument, if the premises are true, the conclusion is very likely true; it is a good bet. In a moderately strong inductive argument, if the premises are true, the conclusion will be true more times than not; in a weak inductive argument, even if the premises are true, they do not give enough strong support to the conclusion; the conclusion is not a good bet. There are no clear boundaries between a strong inductive argument and a weak one.

In everyday reasoning, however, we generally prefer conclusions that are guaranteed, not merely probable. For instance, should a community hire more police to rid itself of a crime problem or should the community rehabilitate the wrongdoer? If the community can only do one, people will want to know which alternative works. Community members will prefer an argument that is logically tight; one in which there is no gap between premises and conclusion. But, unfortunately, the arguments for each solution will likely be inductive in character and their conclusions only probable. The public will have to weigh the evidence for each solution, make the most reasonable choice, and bear in mind that their choice involves some risk. This, of course, makes evaluating inductive arguments more difficult.

Evaluating an inductive argument depends on the particular type of inductive argument with which you are dealing. We will now discuss several different types of inductive arguments and look at criteria for evaluating each. There are four types of inductive arguments that frequently occur in speechmaking:

(1) cause and effect,

(2) sign,

(3) inductive generalization, and

(4) analogy.

Causal arguments are crucial to many different fields in which arguments occur. They are found in everyday reasoning as well as in such specialized fields as science, law, medicine, and business. The public addresses issues such as whether smoking causes cancer; a brochure on AIDS causes people to practice safe sex; TV mediated violence causes aggressive tendencies in young people; and inflation causes high interest rates. Causal arguments

are crucial to these fields because they may demonstrate who or what is responsible for some event, predict some upcoming event, permit us to control events by removing the cause, or explain why something happens.

Causal arguments have warrants that assert the existence of a relationship between two or more events such that one event leads to another. Specifically, every causal argument has at least two events, one of which precedes the other, and both are connected to each other.

Consider this argument:

> The mayor failed to take action on the city's crime problem.
> Since that issue was important to the voters, he wasn't re-elected.

The causal argument above is used to determine responsibility for an event. In this case, the mayor's failure to act is said to have lead to his rejection by the voters. Often, we want to know who to praise or blame for an event, so we ask what someone did to cause the event.

Consider another causal argument:

> We have had more than the usual amount of snow and rainfall this past winter and spring.
> The water has produced heavy runoff into our rivers and lakes, so these waterways have swollen to capacity.
> Another rain will probably flood low-lying areas.

Here a causal argument is used to predict a possible upcoming event, i.e., flooding. The prediction of events, like natural disasters, means that we must first discover their causes. Once we do, we make effective use of causal arguments to alert people of their potential reoccurrence.

Consider a third argument:

> Americans eat too many foods high in saturated fats.
> Eating foods high in saturated fats increases the chances of heart disease.
> So, Americans should avoid these foods.

This exemplifies a different use of causal reasoning. The argument attempts to get Americans to control a possible outcome of eating foods high in saturated fats. Since we know that these foods are linked to heart disease, we can control, at least to some extent, our chances of getting heart disease by eliminating the cause.

Consider this last argument:

> Jane's vision is blurred.
> Her eye doctor told her that cataracts are a condition in which the eye-lens becomes hard or discolored, resulting in blurred vision.
> She reasons that her blurred vision is likely due to cataracts.

The above example uses causal reasoning to explain an event: Jane's blurred vision. The events in the warrant appear directly connected to each other, i.e., an eye-lens is something through which one sees, and changes in it could certainly affect one's vision, and her doctor has already defined a possible cause.

Evaluating **Causal Reasoning** usually hinges on knowing two things: (1) whether the alleged cause was present at the time of the effect, and (2) whether the alleged cause is capable of producing the effect.

In the previous example, a causal argument was used to reason from effect to cause. Reasoning in this manner can be notoriously suspect, unless we know that the alleged cause was present at the time of the effect. Since conditions other than cataracts might also cause one's vision to blur, there is no reason to suspect that cataracts are the sole cause of the blurred vision.

We also must know whether the alleged cause is capable of producing the effect. Let's suppose that you are worrying about making the grades to which you aspire in school. A friend wants to cheer you up, so she gives you a sweater. Each time you take a test in the new sweater, you make a good grade. Soon, the sweater becomes your lucky charm, and you wear it whenever you take a test. Most of us would not attribute the good grades to the sweater. Though there is certainly a correlation between the two events, there must be some basis to support the relationship.

When we establish that the events are connected, we are also required to account for how the two events are related. Such an account depends, of course, on understanding; if you do not understand something, you cannot provide such an account. A causal argument requires that you know what causes something, what results from the alleged cause, how to control or influence it, and how it relates to other events. The core of causal reasoning consists in having a working model of the connections between events in mind as you speak. For instance, the following excerpt provides a "working model" of how infections cause fever.

> Infection is the most common cause of true fever. First, let's take a look at how the body's temperature is kept on an even keel.
>
> Body temperature is controlled in the hypothalamus, a small section of the brain. It does this by sensing the heat of the blood passing through and comparing that with what is called its "set point." Infection throws this off.
>
> White blood cells go into action to fight off the organism causing the infection, and in so doing they give off a substance called "pyrogen." This

acts directly upon the "set point," lowering it to the point that the hypothalamus gets the mistaken idea that body temperature is too low. It then sends out instructions to the body to increase heat production by burning calories.

When you shiver from the cold, the muscle contractions cause the body temperature to rise. This happens in the chill that precedes a fever. Fever, such as one resulting from infection, can be lowered, if need be, by drugs like aspirin. They are "antipyretics," called that for good reason, as you can see. Such drugs return the set point to normal, stopping the heat-production process. (Dr. Paul G. Donohue, "How Infections Can Cause Fever," *Chicago Sun Times*, April 21, 1980, p. 20.).

As stated above, in causal reasoning we must show that the alleged cause is capable of producing the subsequent effect. How is this accomplished? If event A is the alleged cause of B, the connection between events A and B is either **necessary** or **sufficient**, or both. Event A is a necessary cause of event B, if without A, B does not occur. That is, B occurs only if A occurs. For instance, pneumonia is an infection of the lungs caused by a bacteria (i.e., *Diplococcus pneumoniae*). But not everyone who is infected with the bacteria has pneumonia; other conditions must be present as well. So, the bacteria is a necessary, but not sufficient cause of pneumonia. Without it, you can't get the disease, but with it you may not get it either. Reasoning from a necessary condition is a relatively weak form of causal argument because the effect (i.e., B) is not guaranteed by the cause.

Event A is a sufficient cause of B if, whenever A occurs, B occurs (i.e., if A, then B). For instance, a baseball thrown fast at a thin pane of glass is sufficient to cause the glass to break. That is, the combination of a glass pane, having a certain thinness, and an object, having a certain mass and momentum, are sufficient to break the glass. Thus, one can claim that two events are causally related if whenever one event occurs, the other also occurs. Reasoning from a sufficient condition

is a stronger form of causal argument because the sufficient condition guarantees that the subsequent effect will occur.

Sign arguments, like causal arguments, have warrants that also make connections between events. However, in this case, the presence of one event is used to *indicate* the presence of some condition. We use sign arguments to "*read*" our world: a doorbell sound is a sign of someone at the door; a flag flown at half-mast is a sign of the passing of an important person; a fever is a sign of infection; a khaki uniform is a sign of a soldier; holding hands is a sign of affection; wet pavement is a sign of recent rainfall; and a satisfied customer is a sign of a good product or service.

The character of Sherlock Holmes is well-known for tracking down criminals on the basis of signs, called clues. Consider the following paragraph, taken from *A Study in Scarlet* by Sir Arthur Conan Doyle, in which Holmes develops an assessment of Dr. Watson.

I knew you came from Afghanistan. From long habit the train of thoughts ran so swiftly through my mind that I arrived at the conclusion without being conscious of intermediate steps. There were such steps, however. The train of reasoning ran, "Here is a gentleman of a medical type, but with the air of a military man. Clearly, an army doctor, then, He has just come from the tropics, for his face is dark, and that is not the natural tint of his skin, for his wrists are fair. He has undergone hardship and sickness, as his haggard face says clearly. His left arm has been injured. He holds it in a stiff and unnatural manner. Where in the tropics could an English army doctor have seen such hardship and got his arm wounded? Clearly, in Afghanistan." (From A. Conan Doyle, *A Study in Scarlet.* New York: Harper & Brothers, 1892, p.14.)

Holmes uses sign reasoning throughout the quotation. First, he concludes that Watson is an army doctor by observing that Watson is a medical type and has the "air of a military man." Second, he concludes that Watson came from the tropics by observing his suntan. Third, he concludes that Watson has undergone hardship by observing his haggard face and injured arm. Each conclusion is based on reading a sign that indicates something about Watson. Moreover, the combined effect of the three conclusions is a sign that Watson was in Afghanistan!

Consider the following argument based on sign.

> Sue wears eyeglasses.
> Most people who wear eyeglasses have weak eyesight.
> Sue probably has weak eyesight.

In the data something is observed about Sue. The warrant describes a connection between people who wear eyeglasses and their eyesight. Why is this a form of sign reasoning and not causal reasoning? Both make connections between events.

Signs are not causes. From the list of signs given above, it is obvious that the sound of a doorbell does not cause a person to be at your door; a person wanting you does. A flag flown at half-mast does not cause a person to die; old age, perhaps, does. A fever does not cause sickness; germs do. Rather, signs are symptomatic of something. They are outward manifestations that indicate the existence of some unobserved condition.

Some of you have likely noticed a relationship between circumstantial evidence and sign reasoning. In Chapter 10, we stated that circumstantial evidence consisted of circumstances and reasoning. The type of reasoning used in circumstantial evidence *is* sign reasoning. So, there is a close connection between circumstantial evidence and sign reasoning.

Evaluating **Sign Reasoning** usually depends on knowing two things: (1) how reliable the sign is of indicating the presence of some condition, and (2) the number of signs that corroborate the conclusion.

An unreliable sign can only yield an equally unreliable conclusion. For example, in the past the accepted sign indicating death was the absence of a heartbeat or pulse. Later, it was determined that this condition is unreliable. Today, the absence of brain waves is considered a more reliable sign. Usually, signs are reliable when their failure rate is low, especially under adverse conditions.

When a sign has a high failure rate, the strength of the evidence supporting the conclusion is tenuous, causing us to look for other signs that corroborate the inference. For instance, parents worry about whether their child will develop into a responsible member of the community. If, at age 11, the child wants to play a guitar, parents may worry that junior will join a rock-and-roll band, take drugs, and drop out of society. We would probably want to caution them not to be so hasty with their inferences and look for other signs of trouble.

Inductive generalization. In inductive generalization, an inference is made from a subset of a population, called a sample, to the whole of the population. A sample may consist of people, objects, events, or processes, about which something is observed. The results of the observation are generalized to the larger group or population. Consider the following argument.

> All copper objects that we have observed have conducted electricity.
> All copper objects conduct electricity.

In the above argument all copper objects form the population, while the copper objects that "we have observed" comprise the sample. Data is collected on the sampled objects and a conclusion is drawn about all members of the population.

Surveys of public opinion and marketing research for businesses are the most frequent uses to which this reasoning is put. Oftentimes, generalizations about American voter attitudes are based on a sample containing as few as one or two thousand people. The reasoning process uses samples as a means of representing the whole population. But the primary interest of the reasoning lies in the population. The speaker wants to say something about the whole or some portion of the population.

When is evidence adequate to make a generalization? The question has no simple answer, but it depends on two issues.

> Evaluating an argument by **Inductive Generalization** depends on two issues: (1) the size, and (2) composition of the sample.

The exact size of a minimally acceptable sample requires a statistician to compute, but anyone can become sensitive to obvious deficiencies in sample size. Suppose you want to know the grade point average of State U. students and you ask five students for their average. The problem with the generalization is that a sampling of five students is not likely to provide a reliable basis for a conclusion about the student body generally. The size of the sample is too small for such a broad generalization and may prompt us to make a false conclusion about the population.

A second issue concerns the composition of the sample. A sample must have the same grouping of characteristics as the population from which it was selected. If some characteristics occur in untypical proportions in the sample, the sample may not be representative of the population and may prompt us to make a false conclusion about the population. Again, suppose you want to know the grade point average of State U. students. You go to the library on a Friday evening to obtain your sample and ask one-hundred students for their grade point average. Though the sample might be large enough, you should have concern about the composition of the sample. Your sample is likely to

be unrepresentative of the student body because only the most academically determined students are likely to be at the library on a Friday evening. Since the grade point average of these students is likely to be higher than for the whole population, you may be led to an erroneous conclusion about the average of all students. When a sample is both representative and of sufficient size, then there is warrant for inferring a conclusion about the population as a whole.

Argument by analogy. We reason by analogy when we infer that frozen yogurt is good to eat from the premises that ice cream is good to eat and that frozen yogurt is like ice cream in many ways. Reasoning by analogy proceeds from the similarity of two or more objects in one or more features to their similarity in some additional feature. The argument has an unmistakable pattern:

> X and Y share the features 1, 2, 3,…
> X has the feature m.
> So, Y has the feature m.

Argument by analogy frequently occurs in everyday reasoning. When we decide to buy a new pair of running shoes from the same maker of the old pair because the old ones wore well, we infer by analogy that the new ones will wear well, too. When we decide to go to a new movie because it is directed by someone whose movies we like, we infer by analogy that the new movie will entertain us as well. When a child decides to avoid a hot stove because he or she was burnt previously, the child is inferring by analogy that this hot stove will burn as well. Though the reasoning is not often explicit, many of our everyday decisions are based on an argument by analogy.

As with all inductive arguments; the conclusion is not guaranteed by the premises, for it can conceivably fail.

Two criteria of **Argument by Analogy** enhance the probability that the conclusion will succeed: (1) the number of features shared by objects, and (2) the extent to which the features are relevant to the conclusion.

First, the greater the number of features that the objects have in common, the stronger the analogy. Examine, for example, the following argument.

Jane and Sue went to the same high school, took similar classes, and made equally good grades. Jane went to State U. and made all As. So, Sue, who also went to State U. probably made all As, too.

Since Jane and Sue share several features in common, the conclusion is stronger than if they only had the same high school in common. Second, the features, held in common by the objects, must be relevant to the conclusion. Here the weakness of the argument above becomes apparent if the courses that Jane took at State U. proved easier for her than the courses taken by Sue, or if university courses were more difficult to pass than high school courses, the analogy is weak.

Some analogies are thoughtfully constructed, while others are less so. You will need to give careful thought to the unique details of each analogy. Even with many features held in common and all relevant to the conclusion, some analogies will fail at some point. With more knowledge of the subject of the analogy, you discern its weakness. Arguments that rely heavily on analogy are, therefore, vulnerable to objection.

ACTIVITY **12.2**
Identify Necessary and Sufficient Conditions

What is the relationship of the events in List A to those in List B?

(1) Item A is a necessary condition for B.

(2) Item A is a sufficient condition for B.

(3) Item A is neither a necessary nor a sufficient condition for B.

	List A	List B
1. _____	having some water	having some purified water
2. _____	having an FM radio	having a radio
3. _____	having a motorcycle	having a car
4. _____	growing plants	growing flowers
5. _____	growing flowers	growing plants
6. _____	using electricity	using an electric sewing machine
7. _____	having some boots	having some footwear
8. _____	running an electric sewing machine	running a TV set

ACTIVITY **12.3**
Identify the Type of Inductive Argument

Decide whether the following inductive arguments are *causal sign, inductive generalization*, or *analogy*. To determine which argument represents which type, you should analyze the components of the argument.

1. Underline all words which represent DATA once.

2. Underline all words which represent CONCLUSION two times.

3. Write the WARRANT and type of argument.

4. Examine the argument to determine its type and write a challenge to it.

1. "One of woman's most natural attributes is the care of children. Since the ill and infirm resemble children in being physically weak and helpless as well as psychologically dependent and narcissistically repressed, women are also especially qualified to care for sick."

   Warrant _____

   _____

   Type of Argument _____

   Challenge to Argument _____

   _____

2. "Rock and roll is a music form that glorifies the occult and violent, deviant behavior by young people. The most recent Motley Crue and Whipping Girl albums include devil worshiping, women degrading, and sexually explicit, violent lyrics."

   Warrant _____

   _____

   Type of Argument _____

   Challenge to Argument _____

   _____

3. "Television first began to be commonly owned by most American families in the 1950s. Since the early 1950s violent crime, suicide, and teenage pregnancy have markedly increased. Television has caused the increase in these social problems."

Warrant _____

_____

Type of Argument _____

Challenge to Argument _____

_____

4. "That car's tires are in good shape for a used car. So that car overall must be in good shape."

Warrant _____

_____

Type of Argument _____

Challenge to Argument _____

_____

5. "Communism is like a cancer. It requires drastic action and must be totally eliminated."

Warrant _____

_____

Type of Argument _____

Challenge to Argument _____

_____

▣ Building an Argument Speech

The Argument Speech assignment in this book represents a special kind of persuasive speech. Students who are familiar with orations or persuasive actuation speeches will find there are some important differences between the argument speech and these other forms of persuasive speaking. The goal of the argument speech is acceptance of the speaker's argument based on rational thinking. This means that the speaker does not emphasize emotional appeals or psychological strategies as one may in orations and actuation speeches, but relies on logical reasoning to persuade the audience to accept the speaker's claims.

The process of building an argument speech follows the same patterns of analyzing decision factors and making global and local decisions that we have used throughout the course.

Topic Selection

The subject of an argument speech must be a topic about which there are at least two legitimate viewpoints. Consequently, controversial issues such as current political or policy issues make good argument topics. This is not meant to suggest that the only, or even the primary source of good argument speech topics, is the political arena. Nor does a topic have to be an issue that is currently being debated. There are many good topics that may be chosen because speakers want to introduce their audience to a new idea or proposal in the form of an argument. Speakers may explore national, regional, local, campus, and personal issues.

As in choosing any topic, speakers need to evaluate both their own interest and commitment to the claim and the relevance of the topic for the audience. Students often find that local, campus, and personal issues have a natural interest for

both speakers and audiences because of the direct impact on their lives. In an argument speech more than any other speech, speakers must sincerely believe in the argument they are presenting. The presence or lack of earnest conviction will show up in the way the speaker presents the ideas orally to the audience. If speakers do not believe in what they argue, it is doubtful they will convince the audience to accept the argument.

Once you have selected a viewpoint that you find interesting and important to you, then assess the fit of the topic to your audience. Following this section, you will find a survey form that may be used to help discover your audience's beliefs about and interest in your topic. It is not unusual for students to pick subjects they believe in strongly only to discover that most of their audience members hold the exact same belief. If you and your audience are already in agreement, there is really no point in giving a speech on that topic. In addition to determining whether the issue you would like to speak about allows you an opportunity to change how the audience thinks or believes, you must also discover if the audience has a reasonable interest in the topic. For most topics, the speaker can increase audience interest in the subject by demonstrating the societal and personal relevance of the subject to the audience.

In summary, be sure you select a topic that is:

(1) argumentative, as opposed to informative, in nature,

(2) one that you sincerely believe in,

(3) one that leaves you room to change the viewpoint of your audience, and

(4) one that is relevant to the audience. Then you are on your way to creating a successful argument speech.

Additional Global Decisions

As already stated, the speech goal for an argument speech is to persuade the audience to agree with your argument conclusion. When you write your Audience Outcome Goals (AOG), you will begin in the usual way, "I want my audience..." Since the primary change is cognitive or behavioral, most speakers will continue the statement with "to believe that..." or "to do..." You then complete the statement by writing the argument conclusion. A typical AOG for an argument speech is: "I want my audience to believe that drinking more than one cola-type drink a day is an addictive and harmful practice."

The next step is writing the tentative **Thesis Statement.** Just as with the AOG, the argument conclusion is the basis for your thesis. Remember that a thesis has two parts. The first part, naming the narrowed topic, consists of the argument conclusion. For example, "Drinking more than one cola-type drink a day is an addictive and harmful practice..." The second part of the thesis, how the topic will be divided or developed, is made up of reasons or subarguments supporting the argument conclusion. These reasons (subarguments) will be the Main Points of the speech. "Drinking more than one cola-type drink a day is an addictive and harmful practice *for the following reasons:* (a) cola drinks are high in caffeine, an addictive stimulant; (b) frequent use of cola drinks promotes physical and psychological addiction; and (c) cola drinks contain empty calories."

Developing and Organizing Main Points for an Argument Speech

The information you read about your topic will help you come up with the subarguments. After you have explored the evidence related to your topic, brainstorm for reasons and then select the reasons or subarguments that seem strongest and most relevant to the claim you have written in your tentative thesis. The reasons you select will be your Main Points. Remember that each of your reasons (subarguments) should be a complete

argument with data, warrant, and conclusion in the form of either deductive reasoning or inductive reasoning. The creation of the complete argument is how we develop Main Points in the body of an Argument Speech. It may be helpful first to diagram your arguments so you can identify the data, warrant, and conclusion. After you have the skeleton of an argument, then using the information from the chapter, construct a complete argument using the correct modes of either deductive and inductive reasoning.

In Chapter 11, we introduced two patterns of organization for complex arguments: **serial arguments** and **linked arguments**. You may choose either pattern for organizing the complete arguments that will serve as reasons to support your major argument conclusion as expressed in your thesis.

Other Local Decisions

In addition to the usual expectations for an introduction (opener to promote interest, presentation of speaker expertise and significance of topic, presentation of plan of speech) argument speech introductions often include information that provides special assistance to the audience in understanding and evaluating the arguments. The nature of argument topics may make it necessary for the speaker to provide definitions of technical or topic-specific terms and background history about the development of the issue. This background information might include necessary explanations or a retelling of how the issue has evolved or changed.

Because data is an essential component of argument, the speaker must be especially meticulous in an argument speech in presenting supporting evidence from credible outside sources that meets the **tests of evidence** presented in Chapter 10. Appropriate source citations, including information about the reputation or basis for expertise of the sources, must be built into the speech and presented by the speaker.

Speakers can strengthen their message and move toward changing their audience's viewpoint by being sure to clearly repeat the main ideas of the argument in their preview in the introduction, through clear internal transitions between each set of arguments, and by a final repetition of the reasons in the conclusion. Because the speaker may be presenting several subarguments, it is especially important to orally remind the audience of how the arguments fit together to support the thesis.

■ Key Concepts

Listed below are some key concepts from this chapter. Test yourself by seeing if you can define and give examples of each.

- deductive reasoning
- inductive reasoning
- valid argument
- soundness
- causal arguments
- sign arguments
- argument by inductive generalization
- argument by analogy
- necessary condition
- sufficient condition

Chapter Study Guide

You should be able to:

- Name the two issues used to determine the merit of any argument.

- Distinguish between *Deductive* and *Inductive Reasoning*.

- Define a valid *Deductive Argument*.

- Be able to apply *Venn diagrams* to analyze the validity of *Deductive Arguments*.

- Explain the requirements of a sound argument.

- Identify, differentiate, and model the four types of *Inductive Arguments: Cause, Sign, Inductive Generalization*, and *Analogy*.

- Be able to apply two tests for each type of *Inductive Argument* to analyze its strength.

- Give guidelines for planning an *Argument Speech*.

ASSIGNMENT
Argument

Length:	Between five and seven minutes
Task:	This speech should incorporate what you have learned about Evidence and Argument. The speaker will present the Conclusion and Data for one major argument The Argument Conclusion will be the Thesis for the speech. Data for the Primary Argument will consist of: Subarguments (Main Points) supported by additional Data, factual evidence, and expert opinion. The presentation will include an introduction that provides the audience with necessary background information and the significance of the issue for the audience; development of the major argument; and a conclusion that reiterates the Thesis. The speaker is responsible for citing outside sources at the time of the presentation of the evidence.
	A common pattern of organization for an Argument Speech is to present the major Argument Conclusion and then present the Subarguments as Reasons for accepting the major argument.
Note Restrictions:	You may use one 4 × 6 notecard if you wish. You are not required to use any notes; however, you are required to hand in either the notecard or a brief outline or map of the plan of the speech at the end of the speech.
Preparation:	You will fill out and turn in the "Speech Planning Sheet" provided for the Argument Speech. In addition, you should practice and time the argument as you plan to present it in class.

Speech Planning Sheet

1. What is the Conclusion (Thesis) of the major argument the speaker is presenting?

   _____

   _____

2. What is the Warrant of the major argument and what type of argument is being presented?

   _____

   _____

3. What are the subarguments that support the major argument?

   _____

   _____

4. Briefly list the Data used to support the arguments.

   _____

   _____

5. What are the outside sources of the Data?

   _____

   _____

6. What is the significance of the issue for the audience?

   _____

   _____

7. What background and definitions are needed?

   _____

   _____

8. How long was the speech in the final practice? _____ minutes

Instructor's Evaluation of Argument

Introduction prepared audience for presentation by defining terms
and providing background explanations _____

Introduction established societal and/or personal relevance _____

Speaker clearly shared major Argument Claim _____

Speaker previewed subarguments _____

Speaker selected a variety of supporting data (subarguments, facts,
expert opinions) _____

Data met the evidence tests (relevancy, accuracy, expertise, recency,
consistency) _____

Speaker cited outside sources for statistics, observations, opinions,
quotations, ideas, organization _____

Speaker presented support for authorities' expertise _____

Speaker maintained audience interest _____

Speaker summarized subclaims or support _____

Speaker chose a closing which was consistent with and reinforced
Thesis and Audience Outcome Goal _____

Presentation moved toward realization of Audience Outcome Goal
of audience acceptance of Thesis _____

Speech met the requirements of the assignment _____

Speakers' delivery worked to support the Audience Outcome Goal _____

Speaker refrained from distracting voice and body behaviors _____

Instructor's Evaluation of Argument

Introduction prepared audience for presentation by defining terms and providing background explanations _____

Introduction established societal and/or personal relevance _____

Speaker clearly shared major Argument Claim _____

Speaker previewed subarguments _____

Speaker selected a variety of supporting data (subarguments, facts, expert opinions) _____

Data met the evidence tests (relevancy, accuracy, expertise, recency, consistency) _____

Speaker cited outside sources for statistics, observations, opinions, quotations, ideas, organization _____

Speaker presented support for authorities' expertise _____

Speaker maintained audience interest _____

Speaker summarized subclaims or support _____

Speaker chose a closing which was consistent with and reinforced Thesis and Audience Outcome Goal _____

Presentation moved toward realization of Audience Outcome Goal of audience acceptance of Thesis. _____

Speech met the requirements of the assignment _____

Speakers' delivery worked to support the Audience Outcome Goal _____

Speaker refrained from distracting voice and body behaviors _____

Sample Speech Planning Sheet

1. What is the Conclusion (Thesis) of the major argument the speaker is presenting?

   The lack of a national program of health insurance results in harm for the American People.

2. What is the Warrant of the major argument and what type of argument is being presented?

   There is a direct causal relationship between a lack of national health insurance

   and harmful effects on American citizens.

   Causation Argument

3. What are the subarguments that support the major argument?

   (1) Mothers do not have prenatal health care so babies die or have poor health;

   (2) Families must use all their financial resources to pay for health care;

   (3) Health care is not equal for all citizens.

4. Briefly list the Data used to support the arguments.

   # of mothers below poverty line who cannot afford health care:

   U.S. infant mortality highest among the industrial nations;

   Examples of families who lost homes and declared bankruptcy because of med. bills;

   Examples and statistics of people who do not take preventive measures because of cost;

   Quote from Surgeon General about status of U.S. medical care for all citizens.

5. What are the outside sources of the Data?

   Time, June 23, 1995; Newsweek, March 12, 1992; New York Times, May 4, 1994

   Journal of AMA July, 1995.

6. What is the significance of the issue for the audience?

   Health costs are going up; everyone is at risk of accident or illness; your present private

   insurance and your taxes pay for lost workdays and medical problems of others.

7. What background and definitions are needed?

   Brief view of present health insurance in U.S.; brief view of status of U.S. health; explain

   briefly national health plan of Canada; define "system of national health care insurance"

8. How long was the speech in the final practice?   6 ½   minutes

Peer Evaluation of Argument

Name of Speaker _____ Your Name _____

Speech Topic _____

Listening For Content

1. What did you think was the Thesis of the speech? _____

    _____

2. What did you think was the Audience Outcome Goal? _____

    _____

3. What did you think were the Main Points? _____

    _____

4. How did the speaker establish audience "need to know"? _____

    _____

5. Which type(s) of argument did the speaker use? _____

    _____

Listening For Evaluation

1. List two examples of evidence the speaker used and evaluate the strength of each. _____

    _____

2. After hearing the speech, how willing are you to accept the speaker's argument? Why or why
    not? _____

    _____

3. What delivery aspect (how the speaker looked and sounded) was most effective and why? _____

    _____

4. Name two things that would have improved the speech. _____

    _____

ASSIGNMENT
Impromptu Argument Speech

Length: No more than two minutes

Task: The speaker will spend about 10 minutes creating a short argument that includes two subarguments (reasons) supported by at least one piece of support for each reason. The speech must also have a brief introduction and conclusion.

Note Restrictions: The speaker may use notes from a 4 × 6 notecard or the student may speak from the "Speech Planning Sheet."

Preparation: Complete the "Speech Planning Sheet."

Speech Planning Sheet for Impromptu Argument Speech

1. Choose **one Argument Claim** from the list provided.

2. If necessary rewrite the Claim.

   Claim I have chosen: _____

   _____

3. Think of at least five reasons why the audience should accept the claim.

   Reasons:

   1. _____

   2. _____

   3. _____

   4 _____

   5. _____

4. Mark the **two best reasons** from your list. These will be your **two Main Points**.

5. Plan at least one piece of support for each of your two main points. You may use any type of support material (narration, definition, description, comparison, evidence, opinion, statistics, factual data]). Remember examples are types of definitions and comparisons. You may also use explanations.

   A. Support for Main Point 1: _____

   _____

   _____

   B. Support for Main Point 2: _____

   _____

   _____

6. Plan a brief introduction and conclusion.

Topics For Impromptu Argument Speech

1. Funding for college athletics (SHOULD) (SHOULD NOT) be equally distributed among different sports (male and female teams, major and minor sports).

2. Underage drinking (IS) (IS NOT) a significant problem at K-State.

3. Same sex couples (SHOULD) (SHOULD NOT) have the same rights and privileges to parent as heterosexual couples.

4. Censorship of books by (PARENTS, COMMUNITY MEMBERS, OR SCHOOL BOARD MEMBERS) (DOES) (DOES NOT) violate freedom of speech.

5. People (SHOULD) (SHOULD NOT) have to have a license to be a parent.

6. People (SHOULD) (SHOULD NOT) be legally allowed to carry concealed weapons.

7. Sex Ed (SHOULD) (SHOULD NOT) be taught in public schools.

8. Medicinal marijuana (SHOULD) (SHOULD NOT) be legalized.

9. UFOs (DO) (DO NOT) exist.

10. The government (SHOULD) (SHOULD NOT) restrict communication on the internet.

11. Standardized tests (ARE) (ARE NOT) appropriate predictors of college performance.

12. Legalized gambling (IS) (IS NOT) beneficial to local communities.

13. The legal driving age (SHOULD) (SHOULD NOT) be raised to 21.

14. Public schools students (SHOULD) (SHOULD NOT) be required to wear uniforms.

15. Alcohol (SHOULD) (SHOULD NOT) be advertised on TV.

16. All K-State students (SHOULD) (SHOULD NOT) be required to pay a mandatory athletic fee.

17. College athletes (SHOULD) (SHOULD NOT) be paid a salary for playing a sport.

18. All K-State students (SHOULD) (SHOULD NOT) be required to take a physical education course for graduation.

19. There (SHOULD) (SHOULD NOT) be a rating system for all TV shows similar to the movie rating system.

20. Standardized exams (ARE) (ARE NOT) given too much weight by colleges and universities.

21. High profile legal trials (SHOULD) (SHOULD NOT) be extensively covered by the media.

22. Students (SHOULD) (SHOULD NOT) have the opportunity to study foreign languages in elementary school.

23. Prayer (SHOULD) (SHOULD NOT) be allowed in public schools.

24. All high school students (SHOULD) (SHOULD NOT) spend a year abroad.

25. The U.S. space program (SHOULD) (SHOULD NOT) receive more funding.

26. All parents (SHOULD) (SHOULD NOT) be required to take a parenting skills course.

27. The new law penalizing underage drinking by suspending drivers license (SHOULD) (SHOULD NOT) be rejected.

28. The city of Manhattan (SHOULD) (SHOULD NOT) provide bicycle lanes in high traffic areas.

29. Federal regulations (SHOULD) (SHOULD NOT) be passed to closely regulate cloning.

30. The government (SHOULD) (SHOULD NOT) intervene in cult activities.

31. The U.S military (SHOULD) (SHOULD NOT) tighten their sexual harassment regulations and the enforcement of those regulations.

32. Violent crime juvenile offenders (SHOULD) (SHOULD NOT) be tried as adults.

33. All HIV positive individuals (SHOULD) (SHOULD NOT) be required by law to register with the National Health Service.

34. The present graduated income tax (SHOULD) (SHOULD NOT) be abolished in favor of flat tax.

35. Women's military training facilities (SHOULD) (SHOULD NOT) be separate from men's facilities.

36. Every high school student (SHOULD) (SHOULD NOT) be required to do community service in order to graduate.

37. Assisted suicide (SHOULD) (SHOULD NOT) be legalized.

38. People (SHOULD) (SHOULD NOT) engage in premarital sex.

39. People (SHOULD) (SHOULD NOT') live together before they are married.

40. TV violence (DOES) (DOES NOT) increase crime.

41. Mosh pits (SHOULD) (SHOULD NOT) be illegal.

42. The internet (SHOULD) (SHOULD NOT) be censored.

43. Marijuana (IS) (IS NOT) a stepping stone to using other drugs.

44. The Greek system (DOES) (DOES NOT) provide benefits to KSU.

45. Same sex marriages (SHOULD) (SHOULD NOT) be legalized.

46. The voting age (SHOULD) (SHOULD NOT) be raised to 21.

47. Democracy (IS) (IS NOT) the best form of government.

48. The U.S. (SHOULD) (SHOULD NOT) have an official language for the nation.

49. The U.S. (SHOULD) (SHOULD NOT) adopt a socialized medicine program.

50. Big-time College Football (SHOULD) (SHOULD NOT) be abolished and a farm-club system like baseball should take its place.

51. Teacher evaluations (SHOULD) (SHOULD NOT) be made public knowledge on the K-State campus.

52. College students (SHOULD) (SHOULD NOT) have credit cards.

53. Alcoholism (IS) (IS NOT) a significant problem at K-State.

54. The U.S. (SHOULD) (SHOULD NOT) continue to support the United Nations.

55. The *Collegiate* (SHOULD) (SHOULD NOT) print embarrassing stories about campus figures on the front page.

56. K-State (SHOULD) (SHOULD NOT) build a parking garage.

57. All K-State students (SHOULD) (SHOULD NOT) be required to sign a non-cheating pledge.

58. Violent criminals (SHOULD) (SHOULD NOT) receive more severe punishment than they do, possibly even the death penalty.

59. Colleges and Universities (SHOULD) (SHOULD NOT) allow hate speech on campus.

60. The United States (SHOULD) (SHOULD NOT) intervene in countries where there are human rights abuses.

61. Public universities (DO) (DO NOT) provide a better education for their cost than private universities.

62. Manhattan (SHOULD) (SHOULD NOT) have a mandatory recycling program.

ASSIGNMENT
Argument Analysis

Instructions: You will be assigned to analyze one argument from a speech given by another student in your class. You may choose either the major argument or a subargument. First record the parts of the argument on the form below. If you are not able to get the information down when you first hear the speech, ask to hear a tape of the speech or ask the speaker to repeat the information for you individually. Once you have the parts of the argument written, go ahead and make challenges to both the Data and the Reasoning based on the section on Testing Arguments.

Speaker's Name: _____

Data: _____   **Claim:** _____

_____   _____

_____   _____

_____   _____

_____   _____

Warrant: (type _____)

_____

_____

_____

_____

Challenge to Data: _____

_____

_____

_____

Challenge to Reasoning: _____

_____

_____

_____

Sample Argument Analysis Assignment

Here is an example of how an argument can be analyzed to fulfill the argument analysis assignment.

The Argument: "College sports are an educational scandal that takes advantage of young athletes. Many don't get degrees and end up unable to make a career out of their athletic experiences. Tom Scates was once the starting center of a winning Georgetown team. He had hoped to make the NBA, but works instead as a doorman at a Washington hotel.

Model of the Argument:

Data:

Tom Scates' college ball career did not end up as a professional sports career. He works in a non-professional job.

Conclusion:

College sports are harmful to players since they do not lead to worthwhile careers.

Warrant: (generalization)

What is true for Tom Scates is true for all college athletes.

Challenge To Data: Only one example is given. That is not sufficient evidence. The source of the evidence is not given nor is the date.

Challenge To Reasoning: Only one example is given. We do not know if this example is typical of all college athletes.

Using the example above as a model, practice modeling and challenging the following two arguments.

Argument: State-U does not have a parking problem. The campus police report that there are vacant parking spots at all hours every day somewhere on campus.

Data: _____   **Claim:** _____

_____   _____

_____   _____

_____   _____

_____   _____

Warrant: (type _____)

_____

_____

_____

_____

Challenge to Data: _____

_____

_____

_____

Challenge to Reasoning: _____

_____

_____

_____

Argument: "The Federal government considers the nutrition in school meals a priority. In 1990, the U.S. government spent 2.7 million dollars on school lunch programs."

Data: _____   **Claim:** _____

_____   _____

_____   _____

_____   _____

Warrant: (type _____)

_____

_____

_____

_____

Challenge to Data: _____

_____

_____

_____

Challenge to Reasoning: _____

_____

_____

_____

ASSIGNMENT
Final Speech

Length:

Between eight and ten minutes

Task:

The goal of this speech is to incorporate what we have learned about Global and Local Decisions into a complete speech that has as its primary focus either (1) the sharing of information with the audience, or (2) persuading the audience to accept a belief or take an action.

The speech will include the following: (1) a well-developed introduction; (2) a body built on two to five Main Points (Main Points fulfill the Thesis but do not extend beyond it) that use a variety of support materials (narration, definition, description, comparison, memorization, evidence, and argument if appropriate); and (3) a well-developed conclusion.

Information-sharing Option: The speech should provide an in-depth analysis of a topic from the speaker's viewpoint. However, the primary emphasis is not advocacy so the speaker will not ask for audience consensus or action. This should not be a report (talking book) but will undoubtedly require outside sources to provide validation and verification. Make it a speech, your own unique speech supported by outside sources.

Persuasion Option: The speech should provide good and sufficient reasons for the audience to accept the speaker's persuasive claim. The organizational pattern used for the argument speech is appropriate here; however, this longer speech allows for greater development of arguments and the opportunity to include persuasive appeals in the introduction and conclusion. Two elements are especially important: (1) speaker's sincere commitment to the topic; and (2) sufficient strong evidence to support the claims.

Note Restrictions:

You may use one 4 × 6 notecard if you wish to. You are not required to use any notes; however, you are required to hand in either the notecard or a brief outline or map of the plan of the speech at the end of the speech. During the oral presentation, you must cite any outside materials used for documentation at the time you present the information.

Preparation:

You will fill out and turn in the "Speech Planning Sheet." Of course, you will also practice.

Speech Planning Sheet

1. What is the primary Audience Outcome Goal? _____

   _____

2. What are secondary Audience Outcome Goals? _____

   _____

   _____

3. What is the Thesis being developed in the speech? _____

   _____

4. How did you collect information to determine what your audience already knows about the topic? _____

5. How did you collect information to determine your audience's attitudes toward your topic? ___

   _____

   _____

6. What is the significance of the speech topic for the audience? _____

   _____

   _____

7. What are your Main Points? _____

   _____

   _____

8. What outside sources did you use as research for the speech? _____

   _____

   _____

   _____

9. Practice time? _____ minutes

ASSIGNMENT
Composite Speech

Length: Between seven and nine minutes

Task: The goal of this speech is to create one speech that demonstrates the student's knowledge of and skills in using the major speech building topics covered in this course: global decisions, local decisions, a variety of support materials, the structure and presentation of an audience-centered speech.

The speech must meet the following requirements:

(1) The THESIS must be a **major argument.**

(2) The MAIN POINTS will be **reasons** for agreeing with the thesis.

(3) The main points must be supported with **at least three types of support material** in addition to argument (narration, definition, description, comparison, evidence, memorization).

(4) In addition to personal information, you must use and cite orally **in the speech at least TWO OUTSIDE SOURCES** such as books, magazine articles, or interviews with experts.

(5) Speech should begin with well-developed introduction including significance of topic for audience and plan of speech.

(6) Speech should end with an appropriate conclusion including review of speech and closer.

In addition to putting together what we have covered in the class to form a complete cohesive speech, successful speakers will put their "own stamp" on the speech through such behaviors as showing a genuine commitment and enthusiasm for the topic, making a real connection with the audience by speaking extemporaneously, adding personal examples or comments, using audience participation, and creating helpful visual aids.

Note Restrictions: You may use one 4 × 6 notecard if you wish to. You are not required to use any notes; however, you are required to hand in either the notecard or a brief outline or map of the plan of the speech at the end of the speech. During the oral presentation, you must cite any outside materials used for documentation at the time you present the information.

Preparation: You will fill out and turn in the "Speech Planning Sheet." Of course you will also practice.

Speech Planning Sheet (Composite Speech)

1. What is the primary Audience Outcome Goal? _____

   _____

2. What are the secondary Audience Outcome Goals? _____

   _____

3. What is the Thesis (Major Argument) being developed in the speech? _____

   _____

4. How did you determine audience knowledge and attitudes about your topic when you were preparing the speech? _____

   _____

5. What is the significance of topic for the audience? _____

   _____

6. What are your Main Points (Reasons for accepting thesis)? _____

   _____

7. What support materials did you use besides argument? _____

   _____

8. What outside sources did you use as research for the speech? _____

   _____

9. What do you plan to do to make the speech uniquely your own or to draw audience into speech? _____

   _____

   _____

   _____

10. Practice time? _____ minutes

Instructor Evaluation of Final or Composite Speech

Speaker aroused curiosity, prepared audience during opener _____

Speaker established an appropriate audience "need to know" _____

Speaker clearly shared Thesis and preview of Main Points _____

Thesis and Main Points are mutually inclusive _____

Speaker selected a variety of appropriate support materials (narration, definition, description, comparison, evidence using fact or opinion, argument) _____

Speaker cited outside sources for statistics, observations, opinions, quotations, ideas, organization _____

Speaker maintained audience interest _____

Speaker presented information that increased audience's understanding (appropriate level of difficulty, novelty) _____

Speaker used strategies to help audience remember elements of message _____

Speaker presented obvious transitions between main points in body _____

Speaker summarized main points _____

Speaker chose a closing that was consistent with and reinforced Thesis and Audience Outcome _____

Speech moved toward realization of Audience Outcome Goal (understanding, appreciation, entertainment, persuasion) _____

The speech met the requirements of the assignment _____

Speaker maintained a natural, conversational delivery style _____

Speaker used voice and body to increase understanding and interest _____

Speaker refrained from distracting voice and body behaviors _____

Speaker maintained eye contact _____

Speaker projected confidence _____

Instructor Evaluation of Final or Composite Speech

Speaker aroused curiosity, prepared audience during opener   _____

Speaker established an appropriate audience "need to know"   _____

Speaker clearly shared Thesis and preview of Main Points   _____

Thesis and Main Points are mutually inclusive   _____

Speaker selected a variety of appropriate support materials (narration, definition, description, comparison, evidence using fact or opinion, argument)   _____

Speaker cited outside sources for statistics, observations, opinions, quotations, ideas, organization   _____

Speaker maintained audience interest   _____

Speaker presented information that increased audience's understanding (appropriate level of difficulty, novelty)   _____

Speaker used strategies to help audience remember elements of message   _____

Speaker presented obvious transitions between main points in body   _____

Speaker summarized main points   _____

Speaker chose a closing that was consistent with and reinforced Thesis and Audience Outcome   _____

Speech moved toward realization of Audience Outcome Goal (understanding, appreciation, entertainment, persuasion)   _____

The speech met the requirements of the assignment   _____

Speaker maintained a natural, conversational delivery style   _____

Speaker used voice and body to increase understanding and interest   _____

Speaker refrained from distracting voice and body behaviors   _____

Speaker maintained eye contact   _____

Speaker projected confidence   _____

Peer Evaluation of Final Speech

Evaluator _____ Speaker _____

Record the following information about the speech just from hearing the speech.

1. What was the relevance of the topic for the audience?

2. What was the Thesis?

3. What were the Main Points?

4. Name the different types of Support Material you heard.

Judge whether the speaker did each of the following at a satisfactory level.

1. Did the speaker clearly share the Thesis and Preview of Main Points?

2. Did the speaker use a variety of Support Materials?

3   Did the speaker cite sources in an appropriate manner?

4. Did the speaker present obvious transitions between Main Points of Body?

5. Did the speaker summarize Main Points in conclusion?

What do you suggest the speaker change about the speech?

Peer Evaluation of Final Speech

Evaluator _____   Speaker _____

Record the following information about the speech just from hearing the speech.

1. What was the relevance of the topic for the audience?

2. What was the Thesis?

3. What were the Main Points?

4. Name the different types of Support Material you heard.

Judge whether the speaker did each of the following at a satisfactory level.

1. Did the speaker clearly share the Thesis and Preview of Main Points?

2. Did the speaker use a variety of Support Materials?

3   Did the speaker cite sources in an appropriate manner?

4. Did the speaker present obvious transitions between Main Points of Body?

5. Did the speaker summarize Main Points in conclusion?

What do you suggest the speaker change about the speech?

Peer Evaluation of Final Speech

Evaluator _____ Speaker _____

Record the following information about the speech just from hearing the speech.

1. What was the relevance of the topic for the audience?

2. What was the Thesis?

3. What were the Main Points?

4. Name the different types of Support Material you heard.

Judge whether the speaker did each of the following at a satisfactory level.

1. Did the speaker clearly share the Thesis and Preview of Main Points?

2. Did the speaker use a variety of Support Materials?

3 Did the speaker cite sources in an appropriate manner?

4. Did the speaker present obvious transitions between Main Points of Body?

5. Did the speaker summarize Main Points in conclusion?

What do you suggest the speaker change about the speech?

ASSIGNMENT
Report on Outside Speech #3: Analysis of Entire Speech

This report will be based on a live speech (not taped, television or radio) which you will have experienced no more than a month prior to the date the assignment is due. The speech you analyze should last at least 15 minutes. Possible live speeches include classroom lectures (not in this class), sermons or homilies, guest speakers at organizations or public forums, work-related training lectures or motivational speeches.

There are, of course, other possibilities. You may not use a student speech from a class. The report should be typed. Your paper needs to be long enough to do a thorough job of Parts I, II, III.

PART I

You will *analyze* and *evaluate* each of the following speech areas. You need to include examples and observations to explain, illustrate, and support your judgements.

1. Credibility of the **Speaker** based on background and experience. You may include background information available to the public and your own personal knowledge of the speaker.

2. Speaker's planning and adaptation related to the **Setting** (location, time of day, size of room, special physical problems in the room, such as temperature, visibility of speaker).

3. Characteristics of the **Audience** which impact on speaker decisions and how the speaker adapted to audience factors: number of people present, reasons why they have chosen to attend, level of enthusiasm for speaker and speech, degree of similarity of audience members (same age? gender? level of education? job or career experiences?).

4. Effectiveness of **Global Decisions** (both decisions the speaker made while planning the speech and how those decisions were communicated to the audience).

   Topic: stated topic, narrowed topic, fit of topic to audience, occasion and speaker.

   Audience Outcomes: fit of primary Audience Outcome, stated by speaker or assumed from context, for audience and occasion; primary Outcome you experienced; fit of secondary Outcomes, either stated or experienced, for audience and occasions.

   Thesis: appropriateness and clarity of Thesis (Theses) either stated or extracted from speech by you; appropriateness and clarity of speech plan or approach speaker chose to develop topic.

   Main Points: appropriateness and clarity of Main Points either stated or extracted from speech by you (wording strategies used to label Main Points, mutually inclusive relationship of Main Points to Thesis).

5. Effectiveness of **Support Materials** *(Narration, Definition, Description, Comparison, Memory Strategies, Evidence, Argument, Emotional and Psychological Appeal)*: appropriateness of support material choices for interest, understanding, memory; strength and validity of support materials chosen; variety of materials used.

6. Effectiveness of **Delivery** *(clarity, reinforcement of verbal messages, comfort of audience, impact on interest, impact on Audience Outcome Goals)*.

PART II

Make an overall judgement of the speech you saw and heard. Explain and support your judgement. You may refer back to your earlier analysis of specific elements and include other elements or relationships of elements that influenced your evaluation of the speech event.

PART III

Tell how your analysis and evaluation of this speech is different than it would have been at the beginning of the semester.

APPENDIX A
Speech Delivery

This text does not include extensive instruction on how to deliver a speech because of the belief that if a speaker:

1. genuinely wants to share a message with the audience,

2. is sincerely enthusiastic about his or her message, and

3. knows the content of the speech well, then the delivery of the message pretty well takes care of itself.

Most people in ordinary conversation have the necessary delivery skills to share their meaning with others. Consequently, we begin the course with speeches that are somewhat like everyday conversation, expecting that students will be able to speak in front of the class in much the same way that they talk to family or friends across the dinner table. But, as you well know, standing in front of a room and speaking continuously all by yourself for several minutes is not quite the same as trading remarks with people you know well in a home-like setting.

In this section, we will explore two approaches to help speakers make the change from delivery of informal conversation to delivery of public speeches. The first approach is based on (1) what the speaker does; the second on (2) what the speaker tries to avoid doing.

Positive Delivery Elements

One of the major differences between delivery of casual conversation and public speaking is the deliberate awareness of, and adaptation for, the audience. Consequently, a good place to begin discussing positive delivery elements is by thinking about how an effective speaker looks and sounds to the audience.

Audience Connection

First, an audience wants to see and hear a speaker who is speaking *with* them, not *at* them. If the speaker is truly in a communication loop with the audience, the speaker's voice, eyes, and body will seem to send out invisible threads that continuously connect speaker and audience. Speakers cannot connect with their audience if they are totally focusing on what they will say next or if they are concentrating on worrying about how they look and sound.

True interactive speech delivery begins within the mind of the speaker. The speaker should think of the speech as a conversation with the audience rather than a performance. The speaker should try to put emphasis on the audience rather than on the self.

Maintaining genuine eye contact with the audience is the most significant means of connecting with an audience. Avoiding eye contact with the audience makes the audience feel excluded and isolated from the speaker. Just glancing up from the notecard and looking in the direction of the audience is not enough. The speaker needs to briefly lock eyes for a few seconds with individual audience members. The speaker should look at the faces in all areas of the room, but avoid a mechanical motion that sweeps across the audience left to right and back again. When speakers really look at the audience, then the audience plays an active role in the communication by sending feedback to the speaker. The speaker can in turn respond to the feedback and complete the circle of communicating with the audience.

Helping the Audience

Audiences want to listen to speakers who make the reception of the message easy for the audience members. This means that the audience can see, hear, and understand what the speaker is doing and saying without extraordinary effort. Consequently, speakers need to plan to stand so that the audience can see their faces and gestures without having to strain. Speakers need to be sure they talk loudly enough and with clear articulation so that the audience members can receive the words effortlessly.

Understanding the speaker's message begins by being able to hear and see the speaker; however, understanding is also enhanced by the speaker's frequent and appropriate use of facial expressions and gestures. When these nonverbal aspects of communication reinforce the speaker's words, the audience gets a more complete message than the message of the words alone.

Speakers can also give their audience a break by including movement that underscores the meaning of the words. One strategy you can use to show your speech structure to the audience is to plan to take a few steps between each major speech section as you "move" in the speech from one section to the next. For example, a speaker might begin the introduction in front of the speaker's stand, then move behind the stand for the first Main Point; step to the side of the stand for the second Main Point; and finally back to the front for the conclusion.

Looking Comfortable in Front of the Audience

The final expectation from an audience of an effective speaker is that the speaker will allow the audience to feel comfortable because the speaker *looks* confident and poised. If the speaker is clearly suffering in front of the audience, most audience members will be sympathetic but will also feel very uneasy for the speaker. If, instead, the speaker is enjoying the experience of being in front of the group, then the audience can relax and enjoy the speech.

A person does not have to be comfortable to look comfortable. Speakers need feedback from instructors, friends, and tapes about how well they project an air of confidence. Like most elements of speech making, successful projection of confidence begins in the speaker's mind. Believing you can give a successful speech and being determined to look as though you are right at home in front of the room will go a long way in helping you present a confident demeanor. You may also want to consult Appendix E on the subject of nervousness to find more help in managing apprehension.

Natural Delivery Style

In addition to the three areas of audience expectations for effective speakers that have just been described, successful delivery depends on the speaker using a natural delivery style. Listen to yourself when you are speaking in front of a group or listen to a tape of one of your speeches. Does your voice have the same pitch, quality, and rhythms that it has when you are carrying on a conversation with friends? In both situations, your voice should sound basically the same.

When performing, some speakers appear to use a special performance voice that sounds quite different from the voice the speaker uses in conversation. The pitch may be higher and the rhythm and emphasis fall into repetitive patterns. This often happens to individuals who speak frequently such as ministers, teachers, and competitive speakers. Once these performance patterns are set, it is very difficult to change the vocal habits. So it is best to adopt a style from the beginning that is basically conversational in nature. It is difficult for an audience to take in the speaker's meaning when they are distracted by strange rhythms or emphasis.

The body of the speaker should also look relaxed and movements should appear to be spontaneous. This means that a speaker should not plan and practice specific gestures and facial expression but let spontaneous movements that accompany the thoughts and words simply occur. Some speakers have a life-long habit of using many gestures; others rarely move their hands. Either pattern is fine. When speakers intuitively create pictures in the air with their hands that further explain and emphasize the words, the audience interest and understanding are both enhanced.

■ Negative Delivery Elements

It is more difficult to give advice for addressing delivery behaviors that a speaker should avoid than to generally describe positive behaviors. This is true because not all speakers have significant distracting behaviors and the specific behaviors of speakers vary from individual to individual.

All speakers have personal habits that add "noise" to the presentation, but most distracting behaviors that occur infrequently and/or are of short duration are overlooked by the audience. For the most part, audiences edit out "a's" and "um's" unless the speaker inserts them in almost every sentence. Some repetitive or random movements of the speaker that do not go with the verbal

messages are ignored by the audience, but when the speaker is constantly rocking or jiggling one hand, the audience may begin to notice. The key to determining if a behavior has become excessive is if audience members are paying more attention to the distracting behavior than they are to the speaker's ideas and words.

Nobody sets out to fill a speech with distracting behaviors. Many speakers are completely unaware that they are interrupting their own message by how they sound or move. The best way to discover if you are doing anything while delivering your speeches that pulls the audience away from the message is to study the critiques of your instructor and peers and then ask for clarification about comments related to delivery. Also by listening to your audio tape in a neutral way, you will be able to hear elements of your vocal delivery the evaluators have mentioned and possibly pick up other vocal aspects that can be improved.

As you read this next section, you will find some typical distracting behaviors that you may have observed when you listened to and watched others speak. Some of the behaviors may be ones you had not considered as distracting because they represent the opposite extreme of the ones that are familiar.

Distracting Vocal Behaviors

The first group of distracting behaviors are vocal behaviors. Some speakers, especially in a classroom, speak too loudly. The speaker may have the habit of loud speech or may have been told at some point to project whenever speaking in public. A voice that is too low in volume is of course also a problem. Another pair of vocal opposites are based on the rate of speaking. When speakers have a very rapid rate, audience members can usually keep up with the speaker if the articulation is clear, but the listeners get tired because they have to work so hard and fast to process what is coming in. Consequently, the audience may turn off a rapid speaker. Speakers who are too slow and deliberate in their speech also fatigue listeners who "get tired" waiting for the next word or phrase.

We have already mentioned in the section on *Natural Delivery*, the distracting nature of a stylized vocal delivery that gives miscues about meaning through unnatural rhythms or emphasis. Sometimes the rhythmic patterns are the same in every sentence and have a hypnotic effect on the audience.

The final vocal distractors are those words or sounds speakers put in when they are thinking of what to say next. These may be the "a's" and "um's" or they may be words such as "okay" at the beginning of every sentence.

Distracting Body Behaviors

Many distracting body movements grow out of the speaker's need to release excess energy, perhaps generated by the excitement of being in front of the group and speaking. You are familiar with speakers who constantly move their hands in meaningless patterns, shift weight back and forth, or stride about the room without apparent reason.

However, a speaker who is too stationary can also cause an audience to mentally leave the speaker's message. Attention wanders when the audience does not have something interesting to watch or when the audience must hold their muscles in one position because the speaker stays in one place.

Changing Distracting Behaviors

The first step to reducing distracting behaviors is obviously to become aware of what you are doing that may bother the audience. As mentioned above, feedback from those who watch and listen to you as a speaker is the starting point. Some behaviors can be changed fairly easily by simply recognizing that a change needs to be made, making up your mind to alter the behaviors, and

then monitoring yourself. For example, changing voice volume can be changed rather easily and quickly.

Other behaviors require enormous attention and effort because they are such an integral part of the person's communication. It is probably a good idea to concentrate on just one major delivery behavior change at a time. In deeply ingrained and fairly subtle behaviors such as using the thinking word "okay," just self-monitoring may not be enough. Additional feedback from others and video or audiotaping may be necessary to supplement the speaker's own observations.

Steps for Changing Distracting Behavior
1. The speaker *recognizes* the problem.
2. The speaker *decides* to change the behavior.
3. The speaker *makes* the change.
4. The speaker *monitors* the change.

The speaker may not be able to completely eradicate a behavior but may be able to reduce the frequency. This will probably be enough, and the speaker should be satisfied with the changes. Don't make the mistake of becoming so concerned about "perfect" delivery, free from all distracting acts, that you lose the focus on message and audience, or become stiff and self-conscious in appearance while speaking. When a speaker is deeply committed to sharing a message with an audience, many of the distracting behaviors disappear by themselves.

APPENDIX B
Dealing with Nervousness

Before students take a public speaking class, it is very common for them to talk about being nervous when speaking in front of a group. Some students dread the prospect of having to stand and speak to a group so much that they postpone taking the speaking class as long as they can. The fear of speaking in public is considered a form of communication apprehension called **Performance Anxiety**. It ranges from a mild excitement about the uncertainty of what will happen when the speaker is presenting a speech to an audience, to fear so strong that it virtually immobilizes the speaker. In this section, we will first introduce some (1) comforting facts about performance anxiety, and then (2) some strategies to help speakers deal with their performance anxiety.

Comforting Facts about Performance Anxiety

1. If you are nervous about speaking in public, you are not alone.

In the past, students in this public speaking course have been asked about their reaction to speaking in public. Two-thirds to three-fourths of the students have indicated that they have some anxiety about speaking in public. The frequency of communication apprehension follows the pattern of a bell-shaped curve. At one end of the curve is the small percentage of people who experience severe apprehension; at the other end are the rare people who never experience any anxiety when communicating. Most people are found under the large dome in the center since most people experience some level of apprehension in communication

situations. Talk with the other students in your section. You will probably discover that they also have their concerns about this new performance situation.

2. The audience is often unaware that a speaker is feeling anxiety.

Don't be surprised if someone in your class gives an excellent speech, looks very poised and confident, sits back down, and then says, "I was so nervous." Even though speakers may be feeling their hearts beat wildly and their knees shaking, the audience frequently will not detect those physical manifestations of anxiety. Some speakers become overly sensitive about what their body does when they speak; consequently, they assume that since they are well aware of how their body responds to their apprehension, they believe everyone in the audience is equally aware. In their minds, fairly normal behaviors seem much larger and more obvious than they really are. In most cases, the audience is not close enough to see every small move a speaker's body makes. Also, the audience may be concentrating on what the speaker is saying to the extent that they miss subtle nonverbal behaviors. There is a good chance that even though you know you are nervous about speaking, the audience will not notice your body's reactions to apprehension.

3. Speakers can give successful speeches even though they are anxious.

As was indicated above, the majority of students in public speaking class experience some level of performance anxiety, yet almost all class members will successfully complete their speeches. People can face situations they fear and go through them successfully. You may know someone who is apprehensive about driving in rush hour traffic in a metropolitan area. Even though the situation is very stressful when the driver has no choice, the driver can make it through the experience. Some speakers discover that once they have started speaking, giving a speech in front of a group really isn't so bad, and the extra surge of adrenaline that a speaker feels may even help the energy level of the presentation.

4. **For most speakers, anxiety becomes less of a problem as they give more speeches.**

At the end of the course, students are frequently surprised to discover that their apprehension has decreased significantly. They may not have even noticed when they stopped being preoccupied with anxiety about speaking and started to look at presenting a speech as just another assignment. The degree to which anxiety decreases varies from student to student. You may be one of the fortunate ones who discovers that working with an audience is fun for you and you just don't have to worry any more about anxiety. Or it is possible even at the end of the course that you will still have to deal with the demons of anxiety before and during speeches. Nevertheless, it is rare for a student not to experience some reduction in their level of performance anxiety by the end of the term.

◼ Strategies for Dealing with Performance Anxiety

Analysis of Anxiety

Speakers can begin to deal with and manage their nervousness by exploring two factors that influence performance anxiety: (1) the basis of their anxiety, and (2) the situational factors that increase or decrease anxiety.

Anxiety Basis

First, speakers need to discover at the most basic level what it is they fear. When asked "What are you really afraid of?" many students give one of two answers. Some students say they are afraid they won't be able to find the words and will stand in front of the group with an open mouth and no words. Others acknowledge that what they really fear is that they will look foolish and the audience will laugh at them or have a low opinion of them.

When you have determined your root anxiety, then consider how probable it is that what you worry about will actually happen and evaluate the impact if it does. If you are concerned about being unable to find words, it may help to know that temporary silence while the speaker thinks is not a bad thing. The words will come. They always do. Even if a speaker struggles to find a word, one can find an alternative word or go on. Only the speaker knows the exact plan of the speech so a deviation from it does not matter.

Speakers who are concerned about looking like a failure in front of an audience need to realize that audiences generally have good will toward the speaker. They want speakers to succeed. They are not just waiting for a person to fail. After all everyone in a speech class is equally vulnerable. All must take the risk of presenting themselves in front of the group.

Situational Factors

The second area of analysis focuses on those elements of the speaking situation that increase or decrease speaker apprehension. What makes one speaker nervous may have little or no impact on another speaker. Nevertheless, apprehensive speakers in their descriptions of what situational factors contribute to their tension do report factors that fall into the same general categories of factors.

Size of audience is one common situational element that contributes to many students' anxiety. The most common reaction of students to audience size is that they are less tense when the number of audience members is small. A few students express a preference for a very large audience since, in a crowd, individuals and their responses are not so noticeable. Speakers also have divergent responses for their preferences related to the factor of *familiarity* with the audience. Some students find their anxiety decreases as they get to know the people in their audience as individuals and can then see them as supportive friends. However, there are speakers who prefer to speak to an audience of strangers they will never see again.

You may not be able in this class to alter the situation as far as size and makeup of audience is concerned. However, being aware of your preferences may help to forewarn you about speaking situations that will be difficult for you because of audience composition and size.

Some factors over which you can exert some influence are those related to *speaking order*. Many people who are apprehensive about speaking hope that by postponing the time of their speech, their feeling about speaking will improve. Based on what students have told us, the opposite sometimes happens. By delaying the moment of speaking, the anxiety increases rather than decreases. When some nervous students sit through the speeches of several other students, they spend the time worrying rather than being able to listen to the speeches and get their minds off their own anticipated presentation. Analyze your own experience to see if the pattern described here is applicable to you. It is usually recommended that speech anxious students speak either first or second on the assigned speaking day and that they be assigned to speak on one of the early speaking days. You are the only one who knows which speaking position is best for you. Make an honest appraisal and then you may be able to select the best speaking time for yourself.

By investigating the patterns of your apprehension, you may discover other factors that effect your level of anxiety. You may discover that how well prepared you are is an important factor. You may find that what you do immediately before class increases or decreases your nervousness. Think about the times you have experienced the most and the least apprehension when speaking and try to identify the significant differences. Through this analysis, you may just locate some changes you can make in the speaking situation that will make it easier for you to speak in public.

Controlling the Speaking Situation

People tend to fear those things that are unpredictable or uncontrollable. However, there are many things that a speaker can do to reduce the uncertainty of giving a speech. Consider some of the following ways a speaker can increase control over the speaking situations.

1. **Prepare well for the speech.**

Some speakers are justifiably uneasy about presenting a speech for the simple reason that they are not well-prepared. You should start preparing the speech far enough ahead of the speaking date that you will have sufficient time to integrate the speech content into your understanding. When you practice, do so extemporaneously. Memorizing the speech often backfires because the speaker has the burden of trying to remember all of the exact words in order at the time they are most nervous. Thorough preparation should increase speaker confidence.

2. Manage the speaking context to decrease your apprehension.

Based on your analysis, you should choose a speaking time that is most comfortable for you. If you can, plan to use at least one visual aid. During the time you are working with the aid, you will be focusing on the aid and not on yourself. Moving to use a visual aid also gives you an opportunity to walk and relax your tense muscles. Then while the aid is on display, the "spotlight" is moved from the speaker to the aid. You should locate someone with a friendly face and begin your speech looking at him or her. If something unexpected does happen, try to relax and not let it bother you. An audience will admire a speaker who can get back on track. The recovery is the primary impact rather than the unplanned event itself.

3. Manage your thoughts to decrease your anxiety.

It is very easy to talk ourselves into being afraid. You may have had the experience of spending a night alone in an isolated spot. You may remember all the stories you have heard about intruders, escaped convicts, or crazed murders. Every sound becomes a threat. Even silence can hold menace. The next morning you realize the fear was all in your mind. When students think about giving speeches, it is easy to enlarge the anxiety that already exists.

It is a mistake to let your imagination dwell on all the bad things that might happen when you give a speech. The minute you begin to play the "what if" game of speaking catastrophes, stop. Slam the door on the closet of things that could go wrong. Instead, a speaker manages anxiety best by thinking positively about the speech. Expect it to go well. If you are well prepared, your speech should be successful. Talk to yourself in positive ways. Tell yourself, and believe it, "this is a good speech"; "my presentation will go fine"; "I'm well prepared for this speech"; "I've done my best."

When you come into the classroom on the day you are speaking, deliberately seek ways to take your mind off of your upcoming speech. Do not sit down and start rehearsing the speech mentally. You inevitably will start the speech, make a mistake, get frustrated, try again, and then repeat the whole process. This start, fail, start again syndrome erodes your confidence and sets up a failure cycle. Instead, find someone in the room to talk to about something, anything, other than your speech. If you are not the first speaker, really try to get involved in the other speakers' remarks. If you can clear your mind before speaking, you will be fresh and more confident as you begin the speech.

4. Manage your body to decrease your anxiety.

There are several things a speaker can do to increase the likelihood that the body will behave itself during the speech. Try to get enough sleep the night before you speak. A speaker who has been up until 3 a.m. preparing a speech, probably will not be mentally or physically alert or comfortable when presenting the speech at 8 a.m. A tired body is much more difficult to control. Limit your intake of caffeine before speaking. You don't need the additional caffeine stimulation to increase your nervousness. Never try to take the edge off your anxiety with alcohol. A speaker who drinks before the presentation surrenders control and may find the body will not respond when it most needs to.

Moving the muscles is an excellent way to help the body relax before speaking. If you can engage in vigorous exercise before your class such as running, brisk walking, running up stairs, you will find you are both more relaxed and more alert. Just before you go up to speak, stretching and yawning will allow you to tense and then relax your muscles. While in front of the class, planned moves between major sections of the speech, or walking to show a visual aid, allow for a discharge of muscle tightness and help the speaker feel much more comfortable.

Special Help with Anxiety

Most students find that they can learn to manage their anxiety through the progression of the course without any outside help. Nevertheless, students should always be able to go to their instructors to discuss their concerns about performance anxiety. Many instructors ask students on the first day of class to inform them about unusual levels of anxiety about speaking. Instructors should be willing to adjust speaking times to best fit the needs of apprehensive students.

In a few rare cases, size or makeup of audience may need to be adjusted for students who are experiencing extreme apprehension. If you feel this describes your situation, speak with your instructor or the coordinator of the course.

No one should drop this course because of anxiety about speaking. When a student avoids the problem of performance anxiety by deciding to drop and try again another semester, the problem usually becomes greater rather than diminishes. If you feel you would just like to run away from having to give speeches and are about to do so, consult with your instructor or course coordinator about support for helping you stay with the course and succeed at managing anxiety so you can become a successful public speaker.

ACTIVITY **B.1**
Communication Apprehension Discussion

The entire class moves chairs into one big circle so each member can see all the others.

1. Each class member in turn names one physical, mental, or emotional manifestation or symptom they or others have experienced as a result of communication apprehension such as "dry mouth." There will be enough symptoms to go around, but individuals may need to think of several.

2. Class goes around the circle again with each class member contributing a strategy to help manage communication apprehension.

3. Class members either state orally or write three general conclusions they can draw from what they have heard during the class experience.